Lost in Grief

Lost in Grief

A Mom's Story

Karen Frenette

iUniverse, Inc.
Bloomington

Lost in Grief
A Mom's Story

iUniverse books may be ordered through booksellers or by contacting:

iUniverse
1663 Liberty Drive
Bloomington, IN 47403
www.iuniverse.com
1-800-Authors (1-800-288-4677)

ISBN: 978-1-4620-2096-6 (pbk)
ISBN: 978-1-4620-2097-3 (clth)
ISBN: 978-1-4620-2098-0 (ebk)

Printed in the United States of America

iUniverse rev. date: 6/08/2011

Contents

Acknowledgments

Writing a book is never easy. Writing a book about personal tragedy is even more difficult and could not be done without support and kindness. To my husband, Tom, thank you for believing in me and giving me the time and space I needed to keep going. To my children—Corey, Jennifer, and Allison—thank you for being there for me every step of the way. To Uncle Rick, if not for you, where would we be today? To my dear friend Allison Albrecht, you are the one who started it all. In your quest to understand and gain knowledge, you ventured to the library and found a book. If you hadn't read it and passed it on to me, I would not be where I am now. From the bottom of my heart, thank you. To Donna, the first person who ever read my story, edited it to the best of her ability and so kindly referred to me as a gifted writer, thank you for your valuable input, inspiration and encouragement. To all the people at iUniverse, including Lena Burkett, Jessica Stiles, and Sarah Disbrow; the editorial department; the design department; the editorial evaluators; and anyone else I may have missed, thank you for all your help. I could not have done it without you.

Preface

Whenever I thought about writing *Lost in Grief*, I felt real fear. I feared exposure, feared expressing in words what my life was *really* like, feared giving others access to my terror when they had never experienced anything like it. But ultimately, I feared failure. With all those misgivings staring me in the face, I kept coming back to one idea, one simple reason for writing *Lost in Grief*: it *had* to be written.

I remembered how, in the months following my son's death, I searched endlessly for some form of guidance, written material that I could relate to, as I tried desperately to comprehend the changes thrust upon me. There were many psychology books, recovery books, books detailing quite graphically the stages of grief. But I did not want recovery, nor did I want someone to tell me how to overcome heartache. I needed and craved real-life stories. I found the selection to be pitiful. I found no books to guide me in learning how to live with such deep and penetrating emotional pain. The consensus from all the available material was to "heal" and "move on." No one told it like it was. Society seemed too focused on telling me how to *get over* death and what I should do to achieve that end.

I found out firstly, and perhaps most importantly, that there is no *getting over* death. As I told a colleague at the beginning of my heartache, the best I could ever hope for was to one day learn how to live with this pain.

Death is a very stark reality. Death is a part of life, yet it is shunned and seldom, if ever, spoken about. It becomes relegated to the past, where it is expected to remain forever.

Lost in Grief is for me as much as it is for you. It is a mere glimpse of what it is to experience the sudden death of a child. Words seem so inadequate, but I think it is fair to say that no death equates to the death of a child.

Introduction

This is the story about life after death—my life after the death of my eldest child and only son. I wrote *Lost in Grief* for you, the reader, hoping to cast some light on a dark subject. It is a very sad story in which death plays the lead role. I will take you step by step from the moments before tragedy struck to where I presently stand, a journey of over sixteen years. I have included the reactions of others, both family and friends, as they struggled with the enormous task of getting to know someone they thought they already knew. I feel it is fair to say that they may wish things hadn't changed. They are not alone in this thought. I have attempted to provide a glimpse into my new life since I was thrust down a path of incredible resistance, a path no parent should ever have to take. It has been many things, but in no way has it been an easy, steady, forward movement toward peaceful acceptance. More times than not, I have been hindered as I desperately struggled to understand the true meaning of my son's death. My story is not unique, nor does it brim with new and innovative ideas on bereavement. It is, quite simply, the story of my life after death.

> *A wife who loses a husband is called a widow.*
> *A husband who loses a wife is called a widower.*
> *A child who loses his parents is called an orphan.*
> *But in Yiddish, they say there is no word for a parent who*
> *loses a child, that's how awful the loss is!*

> —From "An Orphan's Tale" by Jay Neugeboren
> *Copyright © 1976 by Jay Neugeboren*
> *Reprinted by permission of The Richard Parks Agency*
> *First Published by Holt Rinehart & Winston, 1976*

Chapter One

The Beginning of the End

The morning my life ended remains carved firmly in my mind. It began as an ordinary, uneventful day. No warnings, no whispered messages in my ear, no premonitions that this would be the last normal day I would ever experience. Even now, years later, I try to recall any indicators, any subtle hints of what lay in wait only hours away. Did I miss something? Was I, like everyone else on earth, too involved with life to notice the important details?

The day dawned with the landscape cloaked in grey, the kind of morning that inspires further sleep and laziness. The heavens threatened to open up at any moment, yet all remained quiet and dry. The weatherman predicted rain in the short-term forecast, but the sky continued its dark and silent brooding, much like a petulant, sulking child. Instead of working, I stood pajama-clad in my kitchen, contemplating the enormous task that lay ahead of me. I felt lucky—the other women in the office would have given their eyeteeth to have a day off so close to Christmas. On the other hand, the scheduled office shutdown for the holidays was due to happen in a day or two, so maybe it wasn't all that juicy a plum. Personally, I could easily have used the whole month of December to prepare for that one special day—Christmas.

I loved Christmas. I loved the way we chose to celebrate the day, loved the look of gleeful anticipation on the happy faces of our three children. I loved the smell of turkey as it slowly simmered in the oven, filling the house with the scent of sage and onion. But mostly I loved how we decided to teach our children the true meaning of

1

Christmas. Like most North Americans, we had fallen victim to the commercialization surrounding this most sacred of holidays. We believed that we deserved to treat ourselves in a materialistic manner—the more presents, the better. But as our children grew, it became more and more difficult to fill their wish lists. The same held true for extended family members. I recall spending countless hours traipsing from shopping mall to shopping mall, searching for that elusive and intangible "perfect gift." Unfortunately, funds were limited, and arguments always ensued over how much to spend on someone we saw once or twice a year. Christmas was meant to be celebrated; arguments were best saved for topics worth fighting over.

So we began collectively to search for the best way to express ourselves in a less materialistic fashion, and the concept of "Blitz Baking" was born. It would require untold amounts of energy to perform this feat. Patience, perseverance, and planning were the most important ingredients. In those days, I had energy to burn, and I could not think of a better way to express love, caring, and warmth. We had always done things together as a family; this would be a true display of creativity and cooperation.

As soon as I mentioned the idea, our second child, Jennifer, pulled out all the cookbooks and pored over the pages. "We absolutely *have* to make shortbread, Mom. How about candy canes? Don't these pecan balls sound yummy? Oh, we have to have some homemade chocolates." I could see I'd created a monster. Soon, we had a list as long as my arm. Whenever I thought it would be too much work, Jennifer was there to buoy my sagging spirits by saying, "We can only bake one thing at a time, right? If we do one recipe a day, it will all be done in two weeks." She was right, of course. Only fourteen years old when we began our baking marathon, she possessed the desire and the drive to see this project through to the end.

While Jenn and I created food, husband Tom and son Corey mapped out ideas on how best to present these gifts of the heart. I thought cake tins would suffice, as I was searching for a fast and easy solution. I was amazed when they showed me their prototype: a miniature crate, the kind that used to house Japanese oranges. Remember those? I could not think of anything more perfect.

Our second season, creations from the heart were contained in miniature Santa sleighs complete with Santa at the helm and a red satin bag tucked behind him filled to the brim with Christmas baking.

This year, 1994, marked the third season of manufacturing presents, and all the baking had been completed. Our efforts were to be enclosed in hand-constructed miniature oak barrels. My goal seemed insurmountable and daunting—finish the sorting and wrapping of each chocolate, cookie, and piece of cake by the end of the day.

As soon as Tom left for work, I dove into the freezer headfirst and began extracting buckets of frozen goodies in preparation for the final phase. Hours of work lay ahead of me, but it was nothing compared to what Tom had yet to do. Not as lucky as I when it came to booking a day off work, he had only managed to manufacture one oak barrel, and it needed all the finishing touches applied before I could start packing it. Tom possessed almost superhuman powers when it came to finishing a task, so I did not doubt that he would find the time to complete his end of the project. A couple of late nights would do the trick. *Better him than me*, I thought. But for myself, I vowed to do this one step at a time. Strange how those words would soon become my mantra.

Around 8:00 a.m., nineteen-year-old Corey plodded downstairs looking very much like a bear that had been awakened from its annual hibernation. He wasn't grumpy; it was more like he could use a few hours extra of shut-eye. Being nineteen years old meant that only one thing held more importance than eating, and that was sleeping. But his mission that day far outweighed the desire to sleep in. He strolled directly to the living-room blinds to see what sort of day lay in store.

Corey was big brother to two sisters—Jennifer, then sixteen, and Ally, twelve. I cannot imagine a more devoted brother than Corey. Jennifer, three years his junior, had earned the title of confidante, ally, and best friend. She was a hard worker, driven to succeed, and it was hard to believe all that could coexist so nicely with her dynamic personality. She wasn't perfect by any stretch of the imagination, but she came darn close. Where Corey was tall and lanky, Jennifer was shorter and rapidly leaving behind the vestiges of childhood. Dark shoulder-length hair, big brown eyes—if one daughter required protection from all the boys' attention she was sure to garner, it would have been her. Corey would not have thought twice about becoming Jennifer's personal bodyguard.

Ally assumed the title of Baby Sister—a dubious honor—and was often teased beyond mercy. She was, at the time, still growing and learning about life. Not as dark-haired as her sister, she often complained of how much she hated the stubborn blond streak that always managed to show up in her hair every summer. Ally possessed special abilities at problem-solving and always seemed wiser than her years. She would struggle with her math homework, but when I tried to show her how to work with a division question, she always managed to arrive at the answer while I was still on step two. I would use a pen, but she would use her head. I told her more times than she cared to hear that she feared the power of her brain. Physically, Ally was built along the same lines as a brick house. Forget about trying to tackle or wrestle her to the ground. The only ones strong enough to bring her to her knees were her brother and her dad. Little did I know that emotion would be capable of doing the same thing.

December had always been an incredibly busy month for us, more so than for most families. In addition to Christmas, Tom's birthday fell on the twentieth, followed by our wedding anniversary the next day. Earlier that month, I had decided to throw a surprise birthday party for Tom and asked that Jenn assume responsibility for overseeing the last remaining details. Plans had been finalized, and invitations had been accepted. Two days before her dad's birthday, Jenn called me at work and delicately posed the question to me: could she use her brother's car to finish running errands? Jenn had passed her driver's test earlier that same month, and she was understandably pleased with her latest accomplishment. As with all new skills, she could not wait for the opportunity to be on the road in her own car. The problem was, she didn't have a vehicle. Her big brother did, and it sat in the driveway just waiting for someone.

Corey loved that car, and although he was hesitant when it came to sharing, he could not be called unreasonable. He took great personal pride in the maintenance of it, spending hours washing and waxing it to a shiny gleam. If he could be assured that it would be returned to him in the exact same condition as when it left, he would probably consider the request. Then again, he might say no.

As I listened to her request, I felt my emotions tugged one way and then another. I decided I could not solve her dilemma on Corey's behalf. The answer to that question belonged solely to Corey, and Jenn knew it. I told her I felt if she asked him, he probably wouldn't complain, but he would be the one who decided. She knew, as I did, that he would insist on chauffeuring her around, but it would be on his terms and according to his schedule, not hers. I hung up the phone and returned to my job, quickly picking up where I had left off.

Imagine my surprise when I glanced up to see Jenn standing before me. I cautiously peeked around her to see if Corey hovered in the background. Not seeing him, I returned my gaze to Jenn, silently praising Corey for his grown-up behavior. My admiration was short-lived when I found out, in the next breath, that she had taken his car without asking his permission. The invisible line had been forever crossed, and no amount of justification or explanation could ever right this wrong. She responded to the silent query reflected in my eyes. "He was sleeping, and I didn't want to wake him." I gave her one of those "parental looks," the kind that speaks volumes, and I knew by the contrite look on her face that she quickly realized the error of her ways.

She stayed only long enough to confirm her list of chores and then continued on her way, undaunted and confident that she could appease her brother's concerns, whatever they might be. When she returned home, Corey was sure to be awake and would undoubtedly notice the vacant spot in the driveway. Would he be angry? Would Jenn be able to pacify him, or would they have words? To this day, I do not know.

Later that night, during dinner, Corey informed his dad of what had transpired earlier that day, insisting that his car had suffered damage in some way. He told his dad that it felt as if the front end was out of alignment. His worries would not be assuaged until a promise had been made to book an appointment to have the car checked over. The next day, Tom called for an appointment and arranged for the car to go in on December 22, 1994, the same day I had captured as a day off work. This was the sole reason for Corey's early rising that day.

It had been one and a half years since Corey had graduated from high school, and during that time, he enrolled in college and successfully completed a one-year electronics course. This was the first major step toward his electrical career. He had been working part-time at the same electrical firm where his dad worked. He was the shop boy, responsible for receiving stock and cataloging all the nuts and bolts of the industry while keeping the work area of the shop in an acceptable form of organized chaos. It amazed me to see this area so tidy in comparison to his "typical teen" bedroom.

One of Corey's personal make-work projects involved binding various lengths of wire and tagging them with different colors of electrical tape. Blue tags meant twenty feet of wire, red meant twenty-five feet, and so on. This way, the tradesmen could grab a bundle of wire without having to guess the actual length. The cataloging of wire had just begun and would be completed in the new year, at which time Corey hoped to begin an electrical apprenticeship program.

Corey normally worked on Monday, Wednesday, and Friday, but because of seasonal shutdown, the suggestion was put forth that he could work on the twenty-second, which fell on a Thursday. Corey mulled it over briefly in his mind and made his choice. He decided to pass on the opportunity to earn a few extra dollars.

I remember the contemplative expression on his face that morning as he gazed out the living-room window with his hands clasped prayer-like in front of his body. Had I mentioned my observation of him, he surely would have thought I was making fun of him. As his eyes took in the unfolding morning, his expression and motion slowly changed to reflect his purpose for that day. He needed to take his car in for inspection, and this had to be done first thing.

In front of the Christmas tree lay a rather untidy conglomeration of wires and metal boxes fastened to a large piece of roughly cut plywood. It was an electronics project Corey had been working on in his leisure time, and he chose to work on it here, in front of the tree. I nagged at him to the point of pestering to kindly, please, clean it up. To my motherly way of thinking, today would be the perfect day for him to gather it all together and haul it up to his room for further construction and hopefully completion. When he returned from dropping his car off, I broached the topic of project relocation. His reply of "Yeah, sure, Mom" told me directly what he thought of my idea.

Why do parents, especially mothers, feel it is their job to motivate their children? For myself, I assumed the responsibility of coming up with constructive ideas that would result in a positive release of energy and a clean house to boot. As if I didn't have enough to do, I took it upon myself to meddle in Corey's affairs that day, not realizing for a moment that he could think and do for himself. I would much rather have had him in the kitchen wrapping chocolates and making productive use of his time instead of calmly reading his adventure novel. No matter what I said or offered to do that day, nothing would bump him off his comfortable perch. Many times I asked if he wanted or needed a ride to work, and each query was met with the same indifferent answer: "No thanks, Mom." This blatant display of laziness felt like a direct challenge to my parenting skills as my level of frustration increased. How could he just lay around when I had so much work to do? Couldn't he see I needed help? Did I have to do *everything* on my own? If I had acted more like an adult and less like a spoiled child and simply asked him for help, he would have given it, though grudgingly. But I never asked, and he never offered.

Ally, who had been lingering in the background, very quickly picked up on my disappointment regarding the obvious lack of enthusiasm I received from her brother. She joined me at the counter, and as we continued with the chore of wrapping chocolates, cake, and cookies, she commented, "Corey should really get a life."

I stopped, my protective maternal instinct instantly flaring to the forefront. I asked that she look me in the eye as I said, "Your brother has a life. He has a very good life." I then lowered my voice and quietly reprimanded her. "Don't be saying such things. Corey is a very sensitive, very quiet young man. I don't want you saying something you will later regret."

I have no idea why I spoke those words. Perhaps I felt my own nonstop pestering had done enough damage. Ally hung her head and said she was sorry. I told her it would be nice if she apologized to her brother for saying something so rude and heartless.

As time dragged on through the afternoon, the grey skies began to darken with the approach of evening. Corey entered the kitchen and told me it was time to pick up his car. I fumed further. Couldn't he see that I was in the middle of all this mess, and soon I would have to start dinner? I glanced at him as he silently stood there, but he was not one to take my sullen mood seriously. He knew I would drive him, if only because he had asked me. As I prepared to leave the house at 4:10 p.m., I muttered, "I *don't* want to do this." I truly didn't. He exited the house ahead of me and never looked back.

As I drove, we barely spoke a word, lost in our own private thoughts. I wonder now what his were. I pulled to a stop across from the garage. He lingered briefly. Then, as he prepared to hop out, he let me know that whatever the reason for my anxious state, he was grateful and appreciated the time it took for me to help him. He turned to me and said, "Thanks very much, Mom."

The ice around my heart promptly melted. How could I be so heartless? I regretted my behavior, feeling so childish and immature. Before he got too far, I replied, "See you later, Cor." I knew at that moment, he forgave me, and I forgave him.

I thought to ask him when he would be home for supper, but I stopped myself. After suffering an overworked, stressed-out parent all day, freedom from home probably felt good. He would be home when he got there, and he was fully aware of when dinner would be served. I watched as he stuffed his hands into the pockets of his jeans and sauntered away to check on the status of his car. For some reason, I kept him in my sight until he vanished around the corner. I sighed deeply as I eased the car forward and pointed it in the direction of home.

Chapter Two

So, Who is Corey?

Corwin James Richard Frenette, or Corey, was born October 13, 1975, in Kenora, Ontario—Thanksgiving Day in Canada. He arrived ten weeks premature and weighed two pounds fifteen-and-a-half ounces. For someone so tiny, he did not take long to fill my life. From the moment he entered the world, he was more than my child. He was the center of my universe.

Shortly after giving birth, I was informed by the doctor that my precious new baby could not be expected to survive. I remember the shock and horror I felt upon hearing those words, but somewhere, something told me this would not happen. I hadn't set eyes upon my son, but I instinctively knew he would fight to live, and I would stand right alongside him to ensure he survived and thrived.

The doctor prepared for the transfer of my newborn to a neonatal unit two hundred kilometers west of where we lived, and Corey remained there until his discharge seven weeks later. My maternal instincts tore at the thought of him leaving the hospital without me that night, but I knew he stood a much better chance of survival in a bigger city center. So that night, I gave my consent for Corey to leave, but not before demanding that I see him before he left, to assure both of us that things would be fine.

The next seven weeks tested my strength and resolve to no end. The routine became quickly established: three times a week, I would call the hospital and speak with the nurse to chart the progress of our son. On the weekends, Tom and I would drive up to spend every possible minute bonding with Corey, and when we were allowed, we held him. On Sundays, when it was time to depart and return home, we were always the last ones to leave when visiting hours ended. Corey gained weight, learned to drink from a bottle, and eventually came home. Only when we arrived home and tucked him safely in his bassinet did I feel that at long last, we were a family.

When Corey turned four years old, we decided to move to the west coast of Canada, before he entered public school the following year. From my own personal experience, I knew that a move would be easiest on the children before rather than after they had started school. We sold our home, packed up our belongings, and headed for British Columbia. We settled in Nanaimo on Vancouver Island, an idyllic community situated on the water and surrounded by West Coast firs, maples, salt water, fresh water, waterfalls, hiking trails, public beaches and parks, and campgrounds. Mostly, it offered an escape from the hectic life on the mainland. Nanaimo became our city by default; we had originally planned to settle in Victoria, but lack of work and affordable housing prompted us to head north. Tom's sister lived about forty-five minutes north of Nanaimo and took it upon herself to find a home for us to rent. Good thing, too, because housing was in short supply. We arrived in our new city of sixty thousand people (about six times that of our former town), set up housekeeping, and decided to stay.

The years flew by too quickly. We struggled financially for many years; there never seemed to be enough money left over at the end of the bills for extravagances of any kind. We found ways to work around the things that did cost money. We pledged to ourselves and to our growing family that no matter what, we would always be there for each other.

Our world became perfect. We had a son to carry on the family name, a younger sister for Corey to bond and grow with, and finally, a new baby girl to spoil to our hearts' content. It couldn't possibly get any better than this, and it didn't. Those years, we felt complete and whole.

Corey led a quiet life. He was slight in stature; his nature was shy and introverted. He seemed to have a very difficult time trusting anyone outside his own immediate circle of family. When the time came for him to wear braces and glasses, he never balked—he accepted this as part of who he was. He kept to himself, and if someone wanted to play with him or be his friend, they weren't accepted until he felt they could be trusted.

Our lives settled into a comfortable routine. During the week, we did what every other family on earth does, but on weekends, we broke the mold. Saturdays were a free-for-all—the kids could play or have a sleepover, whatever their hearts desired. Sundays, however, were special. No matter what the weather, we would bundle all three of the kids up and head to a park for a picnic dinner, or hike for hours until we could walk no more. Corey loved the woods and always scooted ahead of us, guiding us along, encouraging us to follow. Grasped firmly in his hand was his trusty walking stick, which he whooshed from side to side, smacking down any vegetation that threatened to block the path he sought to forge. We called him our trailblazer.

With few close friendships, Corey turned to his family, and the bond that developed between him and Jennifer would strengthen until they became inseparable. When Jennifer reached kindergarten age, Corey warmly welcomed her to his school, for now he had someone he could count on. He protected her, and the two of them could be found playing together in far-off corners of the playground or sharing a private conversation, their bodies huddled close together in an effort to keep what they were saying only to themselves. Those years soared by, and before we knew it, Corey had completed elementary school and moved on to the bigger world of high school. It would be three years before Jennifer joined him.

During Corey's teen years, he never caused us an anxious moment. He was thoughtful and respectful. He cared deeply for his family. He may have been bullied in school, and I imagine wearing glasses and braces would have made him a target for such treatment, but he never faltered; he pushed forward, ever determined to show the world he mattered. Jenn was close by to support and encourage him every step of the way. When he passed the test for his beginner driver's license, he felt a profound and deep sense of personal accomplishment. He realized that a world of possibility had opened before him, and he was eager to embrace it. By being so accepting of what life had to offer, he showed his sisters they had nothing to fear from leaving behind one part of life and stepping forward into another.

It took him almost a full year to acquire his permanent license to drive. Corey never rushed anything if he saw the wait was worthwhile. When he asked if he could use the family van to transport himself back and forth from school, we gave him our blessing provided he somehow found the means to keep the gas tank full. Immediately and without hesitation, he said, "No problem." Eager to put the days of catching the school bus behind him, he began his campaign for employment. He found a job with Tom's boss, and the dilemma of gas money disappeared. His world of possibility continued to grow and fill him with determination and pride as he continued his journey on the path to adulthood. The future looked very bright indeed.

In June of 1993, Corey completed his twelfth year of public education. His pride in managing to wade through an extremely tough academic year made graduation all that much sweeter. It became proof positive that when perseverance and persistence came together as one, the results were worth the effort. As he sat among his peers on the stage, the pride he felt in this most personal of accomplishments radiated from him. Confidence reflected in his eyes, and his body language spoke volumes as he approached the podium when called forward to receive his diploma. He took another step forward on the long road of adulthood, setting an example once again for his siblings. He led the way, and they would follow.

Pictures to commemorate that special day were snapped, and congratulations were doled out in copious amounts. Corey trained his sights firmly on the endless possibilities. His whole life now stretched before him, telling him to come on, come walk into the future and discover all the wonderful things that lay ahead.

Later that evening, the Dry Grad celebration kicked off. Would Corey attend? He chose not to go to his prom because of his shy and sensitive nature, certain that no girl would want to go with him as his date. But that night, he surprised his dad and I when he told us he would be going to Dry Grad regardless of whether he had friends to hang out with. We volunteered to drop him off, and as I watched him saunter to the registration table and sign in, I noticed the theme for the evening. The banner that stretched across the entryway proudly proclaimed that these fine young men and women were charting their futures. With his head held high, his vision firmly fastened on his next step, Corey would allow nothing to stop him from succeeding, I felt sure of it. My heart contracted painfully when I thought of him spending the entire evening alone, but if he didn't mind, then why should I? We watched as he entered the building. Never once did he look back.

When he returned home the next morning, he could barely contain himself. He had slept only a little, as all the activities kept him wide awake and busy. If determination and faith were the only requirements for winning the grand prize of a new pickup truck, he would have won it hands down. Instead of looking at his unsuccessful bid for the vehicle as a defeat, he turned it into a goal. He told us that because of that night, he would one day own a truck.

He continued to babble on about what an exciting evening he'd had while we pressed on with the final preparations for leaving on what would be our last vacation as a complete family. A huge reunion in Ontario to honor his grandmother's eightieth birthday meant relatives from across the country would be gathering to celebrate this milestone. No sooner had we pulled out of the driveway than we noticed a strange silence coming from the back of the van. Corey had instantly fallen asleep, and Jennifer decided at that moment that she would spend the ninety-minute ferry trip snuggled up next to her brother so he wouldn't be alone.

During our time in Ontario, we chose to spend time together rather than visiting countless relatives. We performed our family obligations when necessary, but as soon as a pause occurred between bouts of people bursting through the door to see us, we did everything we loved to do. We went camping and rented a small boat to try our hand at fishing. It didn't take much encouragement on our part to convince Corey to try piloting the boat on his own. He very cautiously hugged the shoreline, but as his confidence grew, so did the size of the figure eights he drew in the water as he banked first to the left and then to the right. Only when he felt comfortable with how the motor operated did he allow his sister in on the fun. Together they laughed, creating one of the most beautiful symphonies ever heard. Jenn begged him to go just a little bit faster, but Corey, ever the responsible big brother, ignored her and continued at the speed he felt was safest. Meanwhile, on shore, Ally begged for her turn, but Corey said, "No, this is only for big people, and you are too little." We played together for three solid days, and I wished those days could have lasted forever.

The campground where we pitched our tents held special meaning for us. Before moving to British Columbia, we had spent many a lazy day strolling in this park, camping in the summer and playing in the water when the temperature soared into the thirty-degree Celsius range. Corey asked me if I remembered the time we walked on a warm winter's day and came across a tiny spider struggling in the snow. I turned my puzzled expression to Tom. Did he remember this? He refreshed my memory of that particular walk. Corey, at two years of age, squatted down in the middle of the road, totally fascinated by this little spider trying so hard to make its way across the icy crystal-covered ground. We watched it, thinking how odd it was for a spider to be roaming around in the middle of winter. Fifteen years later, we followed Corey once again as he pointed out roughly the area where we had observed that stubborn little spider.

Our son proved to be an exceptional young man. I never doubted that life would continue to unfold for him, trusting that I would bear witness firsthand to the wonderful man, loving husband, and outstanding father he would one day become. I looked forward to that time when I would be filled with so much joy, I wouldn't be able to contain myself.

Chapter Three

Decisions and Consequences

About the same time I returned home, Corey would have left the garage, heading in the direction opposite to home. I imagine that once he saw the impossible snarl of traffic on the highway, he would have thought it better to stick to the back roads. If he turned right, a safe alternative to harried and impatient drivers was almost guaranteed. Before steering his car out of the parking lot, he would have switched on his compact-disc player. Perhaps he listened to his favorite song, "Return to Innocence" by Enigma, as it filled the quiet recesses of his car with its haunting melody. As he guided his vehicle along the roadway, he would have downshifted into second gear before bumping over the railroad tracks and proceeding up the hill, which curved slightly to the left. He was a careful driver; his headlights were on and his seatbelt securely fastened. Maybe he was thinking about the new truck he would soon own. Since he'd set his sights on the pickup, delay after delay had dogged his every move. Dead-end promises and setbacks occurred almost on a daily basis. The latest glitch involved a choice between the truck he'd settled on and a newer model for the same price. He struggled with the decision on which one he should buy—the older blue Toyota or the newer red one. But at long last, things were falling into place. Possession and delivery seemed imminent. I can only speculate on how satisfied he felt with life as it continued to unfold for him.

Having ridden countless times as Corey's passenger, I feel qualified in attesting to his driving habits. Even now, I can picture his right hand on the stick shift and his left hand holding the steering wheel at about the eleven o'clock position. His left elbow would have rested lightly on the driver's door. He drove as he had been taught by his dad—keep your eyes on the road, and never let your attention deviate from the task at hand.

We'll never know if he saw the other vehicle bearing down on him. In the aftermath, all indicators pointed to the conclusion that he did not. No skid marks scored the road. He had no opportunity to avoid the oncoming vehicle as it barreled toward him on the wrong side of the road. In the investigation, we found that the approaching vehicle's right side was seven-and-a-half feet *over* the yellow line dividing the road. Were the van's headlights on? We would never know for sure.

The van began its deadly path of destruction by striking Corey's car on the left front fender. The vehicles did not stop despite the near head-on collision that had just occurred. The airborne van proceeded in its deadly forward thrust by driving up on the hood of Corey's car, pushing it backward fifty-four feet before plowing both vehicles into the ditch. But the van was not finished. As it collided with the embankment, it dove headfirst into the dirt. It scooped up the earth like a giant shovel and pitched it in a wild tantrum with a total spread of over twenty feet. I cannot imagine bearing witness to such awful devastation.

While waiting for emergency personnel to arrive, a paramedic who happened on the scene intubated our son. A woman stopped to help as well and held Corey gently, all the while telling him to take it easy. There was blood everywhere. In the distance, the wail of ambulances, fire trucks, and police could be heard. Did Corey hear them screaming? Did I hear them that night?

Upon my arrival home, my biggest dilemma was deciding what to make for dinner. I retreated to the utility room to investigate the contents of the freezer. As I buried myself in its cold confines, the phone began ringing. Figuring the importance of searching out something suitable for dinner outweighed that of running for the phone to answer a silly call, I decided to let the answering machine pick it up. I surfaced from the frozen depths with the brilliant idea of homemade chicken soup. After retrieving my soup makings, I checked for messages only to find that the indicator light was not flashing. In the same instant, I heard Jennifer's phone ring and thought for sure it must be her boyfriend looking for her. After four rings, her answering machine clicked on. Our phone began to ring once again. "Well, it must be important," I thought as I moved forward to answer this rather insistent call. I wish now I had never picked up the telephone.

Chapter Four

From Whole to Shattered

I answered on the second ring, fully expecting to hear the voice of Carlos, Jennifer's boyfriend, on the other end. Instead, a strange female voice asked, "Is this Mrs. Frenette?"

Naturally, I replied, "Yes it is."

Barely a heartbeat passed before she followed with the next piercing question. "Do you know Corey Frenette?"

How strange, I thought. Cold fear constricted my throat with dread and instantly transformed into taste. "Yes, I do."

She asked, "Are you the mother of Corey Frenette?"

My voice was barely a whisper. "Yes, I am."

Before proceeding any further, she verified my identity again by asking, "So you are the mother of Corey Frenette?"

Indescribable fear gripped my heart as once again I feebly replied, "Yes, I am."

She identified herself, and as soon as I heard the word *hospital*, the fear in my mouth and the terror in my heart ignited into flames of panic that spread like wildfire throughout my whole body. I clung desperately to the back of a chair and willed myself to pay very close attention to what I heard. As I listened, the thought continually spun around in my head that from this moment on, my life was never going to be the same. She told me Corey had been involved in a car accident, the most frightening words I would ever hear. Hope immediately flooded into my mind. Of course! Corey asked her to call home on his behalf, because he was not able to do it! He would understandably be in a state of shock. Only five weeks before, he had been involved in a fender bender. That episode rattled him; imagine how terrified he must feel, so scared he wasn't able to make a simple phone call.

However, in the space of a few moments, this fragile hope was shattered forever, beyond salvation. The words she spoke completely destroyed what little reserve I had managed to scrape together. I heard the words "head injury" and knew Corey would never be the same. I worked in a clinical setting where therapists treated people who had suffered head injuries. I began to rapidly accept the fact that Corey would no longer be the same person who existed a mere hour ago, but the prospect of death never once entered my mind. The nurse asked for me to hang on the line because the attending physician needed to speak to me. When he picked up the call, his voice lacked warmth; grave concern coated his words.

"Corey has been involved in a car accident, a very serious accident I'm afraid. He has sustained multiple fractures, with the most severe involving a head injury of which we are unable to determine the severity."

The only words I could come up with were, "You're kidding."

He said, "Unfortunately, I am not kidding."

He told me that the local CAT scan was undergoing routine maintenance, and therefore they would be unable to determine the exact extent of Corey's injuries. Corey would be airlifted to Vancouver or Victoria for the necessary diagnosis and treatment. My mind reeled; how could this be? How, when less than an hour ago, I left him at the garage? How could he be involved in a serious accident, an accident so serious that he faced transportation to another city for treatment? There hadn't been enough time for something like that to happen.

The doctor informed me that although Corey remained unconscious and on a respirator, he continued to try to breathe on his own. The urgency in the doctor's voice registered in my brain as he told me I needed to find my way to the hospital as soon as possible. I could not allow the real reason for the urgency in his voice to penetrate the barriers I erected in my mind. I rationalized that admission papers, transfer papers, or papers allowing tests to be performed required my permission and signature before treatment could proceed. I refused to believe that this critical request meant Corey's life hung in the balance. At that moment, I placed all my faith in the medical profession. Doctors would, without question, be able to fully repair whatever damage had been inflicted upon my son. I don't recall placing the receiver in the phone's cradle as I stood there wondering if this had all been a dream. I looked around, and somehow everything seemed different even though it remained the same. Realization suddenly gripped me as I came to my senses, knowing I faced a panic situation. Fear caused me to shake as the cold truth forced its way into me. I'm not very good in emergency situations. I felt myself mentally shutting down as the shock began to register. I knew I could not drive to the hospital. I lacked strength, horribly afraid of what would be waiting for me upon my arrival. So I did the only thing I could think to do—I began to maniacally dial phone numbers in a frantic bid to find someone, anyone, who could help restore my world and dissolve this mounting anxiety. My frozen fingers tried so hard to dial the numbers of people I knew, numbers I thought were permanently etched in my brain. It took several attempts to completely dial a phone number, only to reach an answering machine. I have no recollection of who I called, whether I left a message, or how many times I may have called the same person. When at last I did connect with someone, the lead weight threatening to crush me fell instantly from my shoulders. I managed to reach Tom's boss's wife, but I have no idea what I said to her. I must have been able to convey that a critical situation required immediate attention, and that I needed desperately to find my husband.

For a brief moment, I felt safe and secure. If anyone could help solve this mystery, Lois could. I remember her telling me to keep the line clear so she could call me back as soon as she located Tom. She phoned back moments later with good news as well as bad. She had managed to find someone who could take me to the hospital, but Tom's whereabouts remained unknown. With final words for me to keep her posted on Corey's condition, she disconnected and vanished.

I needed my husband, and I needed him now. This *could not* be happening. I struggled and forced my paralyzed brain to think of where on earth Jennifer could be. Then I remembered that she had walked down to her girlfriend's house in an effort to resolve differences that threatened their seven-year friendship. Despite my faith in doctors, I knew time was of the essence; if I could not reach Tom, I had to reach Jennifer. Thankfully, I had programmed the number into the phone, and I listened to its lonely ring as hopelessness sunk its claws into me with the realization that once again, I had reached another in a long line of answering machines. I began to hang up the receiver when someone picked up the call and said, "Hello?" I asked to speak to Jennifer and waited for her to reluctantly come to the phone. When she picked up the call, I immediately asked her if she could please come home.

"Why Mom? We are just heading out to the mall to do some last-minute Christmas shopping."

I wanted to say, "Sure, okay, that's fine. Have fun, and happy shopping." But I couldn't. Unsure of how to make my frantic need known without causing her panic, I tried so hard to convince her that she should want to come home. I begged and pleaded with her. "Please, Jenn. Just come home, okay?" She continued to ask why. Finally, when I could no longer avoid the real reason, I told her the truth. The instant she heard the combination of the words "Corey" and "accident," she began to moan and sob. I kept saying, "Jenn, I need you to come home. Can you do that? Can you come home now, Jenn?" Her continued moaning and crying drowned out her ability to comprehend what I asked of her. I begged her to please, please stop crying. I apologized for frightening her, but I needed her to please, oh please, just come home. I wanted her to help me make this nightmare disappear.

It seemed I only knew how to repeat the same worn and tired words: "Jenn, I need you to come home now. Please, just take a deep breath and listen to me. Can you come home? Can you make your way here, or do you want me to come get you?" Through her tortured sobs, she said she would be right home.

It seemed to take forever before she walked through the door, but when she did, I felt alone no longer. During the whole time of my ordeal, I had clung to the back of a chair, leaning on something for support. As if I were an infant taking her first steps unassisted, I left the security of the chair and reached to embrace my daughter. I gathered her and her friend Melissa close to my heart in sobbing misery. Melissa asked what I knew, and I admitted the information I received was severely lacking in detail. I told her Corey needed to be airlifted to another hospital for a CAT scan, and no determination as to the severity of his injuries could be made without the scan. I returned to my post next to the phone, making one final attempt to reach Tom on his cell phone. It seemed a miracle when he answered the call; he sounded so relaxed. I was amazed that he could not detect the fear and dread in my voice. I repeated the same words I had spoken to Jennifer. I asked if he could please come home immediately, purposefully leaving out the reason for my request. I also remember telling him to please drive carefully.

What happened in that indeterminable space of time between hanging up the phone and hearing the door close behind him? Did I have any thoughts? Did I move? Did the phone ring? Had he noticed Jenn and Melissa as they sat huddled in the corner crying? Did he wonder why a co-worker of his stood in our kitchen, nervously moving back and forth, not knowing if he should leave or stay? I raised my anguished eyes to his and tried as gently as I could to utter the words that I knew would lead to the complete and total destruction of his world. I helplessly watched as the meaning of what I said slammed into him, as each syllable sank its teeth deeper and deeper into his soul. I watched woodenly as he raced madly up the stairs to change his clothes, returning seconds later with his shirt askew and the buttons mismatched to the holes. I followed his lead as we raced to our car, leaving everyone else behind.

The harried dash to the hospital took forever. It felt as if we were caught in some sort of time warp where everything slowed to the point of almost standing still. We weaved in and out of traffic as if this were the Indy 500 and we were trying to beat some sort of race with the clock.

We had barely screeched to a halt before we bolted for the emergency entrance. Dazed and confused, we looked around for someone to help us. Why were we here? When would this sick and horrible joke come to an end? It took only a moment before a nurse noticed our explosive arrival. She asked if we were Corey's parents. What happened? Where was Corey? She shuttled us into an area off the main emergency room that sorely lacked in privacy. A thin cotton curtain the color of pea soup, ragged and worn, separated us from the rest of the hospital. I tried to rationalize things as I struggled to place all that had happened in some sort of logical order. Would they put us in this area if the doctor needed to deliver some really bad news? What defined really bad news?

By the time we arrived at the hospital, Corey had spent over an hour alone. His car was so badly damaged that the Jaws of Life were needed to extract him from the twisted wreckage. Precious minutes ticked by as complete strangers worked in vain to save our son. For an hour and a half he lay alone, wondering what had happened, confused because he could not wake up, frightened and only wanting his family. For an hour and a half, he fought alone. From the moment we arrived at the hospital, we vowed he would not have any further moments alone; we would remain by his side for as long as we needed to be there.

I watched as an unfamiliar doctor magically appeared, slipping through an unseen opening in the thin fabric that cloaked our world. Why did he appear so blurry and out of focus? Fragments of his speech filtered through my cotton-clogged mind. "Head injury," "stabilized," "lost a lot of blood," "transfusions," "respirator," "contusions," "hasn't regained consciousness and we don't know why," "helicopter for transfer," "you can see him," "hearing is the last thing to go"—all of these phrases came to me disjointedly as I struggled to understand what this man meant. I felt my frustration mounting. Why did he say that hearing was the last thing to go? Go where? When I looked up, the doctor had evaporated as if he were made of mist. We waited, cemented to the tile floor, afraid to move, terrified that we couldn't. Without warning, a nurse ushered us into the area where she said Corey lay.

With lead-weighted feet, I followed her through the entrance stating that only authorized personnel were allowed. Each breath became harder to take as I fought to control my mounting anxiety and fear. When she stopped and pointed, I immediately lowered my eyes. The white tile floor was spattered with blood. I slowly raised my eyes, trying in vain to absorb an image I would never forget.

Corey's motionless body lay on a stretcher directly above the splotched, bright red puddles. I glanced downward again and watched in abject horror as the blood continued to drip. We approached him cautiously, in a state of deep shock, afraid of many things, afraid of this new reality, fiercely looking for a way out. In the same breath, I wanted to know how something like this could happen to us. I looked at Corey's face, his head swathed in bandages and his left eye horribly bruised. He looked as if he had fallen off a building or been run over by a truck. I could not imagine this happening to someone as sweet, as gentle, as kind as Corey. I needed for someone to tell me what had happened to cause him such damage. How did he get this way?

The force of the collision left its indelible mark upon his sweet and gentle face. I assessed the physical damage I could see on his face, the cut on the bridge of his nose where his glasses normally rested. Blood oozed from his nose and his left ear. His legs appeared enormous from the dressings, bandages, and splints. We learned he had suffered compound fractures to both femurs as well as breaks to the lower extremities of both legs. His hands were shattered, his left wrist broken. His jaw was fractured. He continued to bleed internally from a tear to his large intestine. But by far, the injury that caused the most distress was the undetermined, frightening, concealed head injury. Without a CAT scan, speculation as to its severity would amount to nothing more than an educated guess. He would receive a total of five units of blood before his eventual transfer to Victoria, which amounted to all the blood his body would hold. As he lay on the stretcher, he looked so cold. The blood continued to drip to the tile floor below while I tried in vain to reconcile that this poor, broken soul was our son. Just looking at his face should have been all the proof I needed. I searched for further evidence, determined to prove that although this may have looked like Corey, it couldn't possibly be him. I hunted for the tiny scar on his left index finger, the result of a too-close encounter with a pair of side cutters. While snipping a piece of sheet metal, the cutters slipped, and the tin sliced deeply into his finger. To my horror, I found the scar, presenting me with indisputable proof. I ran out of options, I ran out of ideas for proving that the hospital officials, the police, the ambulance personnel had mistakenly identified Corey as the victim of this horrific accident. I had no choice but to accept that Corey lay on the stretcher before me, battered, broken, and bleeding.

A respirator breathed for him, thrust into his airway, his mouth stretched impossibly wide. How that must have hurt. At regular intervals, a deep sigh occurred between the measured whooshes of the machine. During those deep, artificially machine-induced breaths, Corey fought to breathe on his own. Tom placed his hand gently on Corey's cold and naked shoulder as he spoke: "Just relax, son. Let the machine do the work for you. Let the machine breathe for you so you can concentrate on fixing that headache." Corey seemed to respond to his father's words, drawing deep comfort from our presence, knowing we were there with him, that he wasn't alone.

The pool of blood on the floor continued to grow in size. Why? A nurse casually strolled past where he lay, acting as if we were invisible. I felt a wave of oppression descend upon me and knew that if I didn't leave the emergency room immediately, I would collapse. I made the excuse to Tom that I should call relatives. Snapped out of his reverie, Tom quickly agreed. I could not stand by helplessly and watch my son's life drain away. I began to wonder why we were here. Why was nothing being done to help Corey, to stem the flow of blood pooling on the floor? Why wasn't he being transferred, airlifted to another facility? For what in heaven's name were we waiting?

I walked woodenly to the bank of pay phones, angrily stabbed at the buttons, punching in phone numbers. I have no recollection of who I called, who I talked to, or how many answering machines picked up my call. I have no idea how I managed to dial phone numbers; I had no directory, no listing of phone numbers, nothing. Did I call home? Who did I talk to? What did I say? Did I return to Corey's side? When the milky vision of Jennifer and Allison appeared before me, I drew great comfort from their presence. Did I summon them? Did they insist that someone bring them to the hospital?

I noticed the worn brown teddy bear Jenn clutched in her arms, pressed fearfully to her heart. The suffering and unspeakable agony reflected in her soft brown eyes bored straight into my heart. "Please tell me this isn't happening, Mom. Please!"

Ally walked as if in a trance, angry, disoriented, and frightened. Why should they be here? Why should they have to endure this? Why could we not return home, all of us, and eat dinner as planned? When I asked my daughters if they wanted to see their brother, Jennifer instantly agreed, knowing she belonged by her brother's side. Ally, on the other hand, seemed terribly unsure. She feared that the reality of Corey truly lurked on the other side of those heavy official doors. Frightened to face an awful truth, a truth she was ill-equipped to handle, she felt terrified to believe that tragedy could actually touch her family and destroy her trust and belief.

We entered the trauma room. I noticed once again an incredible lack of personnel surrounding Corey. Maybe his injuries were not that serious after all, but now when I think of it in retrospect, there was probably little they could do for him. I recall one nurse referring to the respirator's sighing. "It helps," she said, "to keep the small alveoli inflated and in use. We do it naturally, but Corey can't, so the machine assists him in doing this." We returned our gaze to the stretcher and waited, looking at each other and trying in vain to figure out for what we were waiting. Could it be a miracle? No, I believed the time for miracles would come later. We were waiting for the helicopter that would take Corey to a big medical facility in either Vancouver or Victoria. No decision on the destination had been made.

From somewhere in the depths of this twisted and artificial reality, Tom told me that I would need to return home to pack up our things for the possibility of staying away for a few days. Out of thin air, Bill and Lois, Tom's boss and his wife, materialized before me and said they would gladly drive me home and bring me back to the hospital. I didn't want to leave Corey, but Tom promised to stay with him and not leave his side. The girls jumped at the opportunity to leave the hospital, saying they needed to come with me. I sat in the backseat of the car with Jenn and Ally sandwiching me on either side. My memory of the drive home remains unclear. I remember looking out the car window and wondering how this could be happening. Where had my life gone? Bill pulled into the driveway and said he would wait for my return. I burst through the door, raced upstairs, and began to haphazardly toss clothing into a suitcase. I have no idea what I grabbed. Suddenly, a voice behind me drew my attention from the task at hand. "Mom, Harriet's here."

I turned to see my neighbor standing in the doorway to my bedroom. She embraced me as she said, "My thoughts and prayers are with you." As suddenly as she appeared, she vanished.

"Now why would we need her prayers?" I asked myself. We weren't in an emergency situation where we would need and then seek divine intervention, were we? Prayers were only offered as a last resort. I quickly rationalized that the poor woman had been fed wrong information, but if praying helped her, then that would be fine. I resumed what I needed to do, moving as quickly as possible as thoughts of returning to Corey pushed me onward.

My daughters and I jumped into the car and raced back to the hospital. Upon entering the emergency ward, I noticed two men dressed in jumpsuits standing off to the side. I breathed a sigh of relief when I read the words "Helicopter Crew" on their clothing. But why were they not moving? What in heaven's name were they doing—but more importantly, why were they not rushing Corey out the door? They shuffled their feet nervously from side to side, their hands shoved deeply into their pockets as they chatted amiably. I searched out Tom, and he informed me of the latest delay. It seemed that the splints supporting Corey's broken legs were too long to fit into the helicopter. Adjustments had to be made while precious minutes ticked by.

During this agonizingly slow progression of time, we noticed a police officer hovering at a desk filling out some sort of report. Tom and I walked toward him hesitantly, hoping, yet dreading, that he might somehow be involved. He glanced up indifferently at our approach and asked, "Are you folks the registered owners of the blue car involved in the accident?" We mutely nodded, whereupon he asked if we could provide the missing details on the driver. The accident form lay spread on the counter before him, and I studied it as inconspicuously as possible. I needed to know what would cause such destruction. I gazed at the sketch of the vehicles, desperately trying to make some sense out of it. The cartoon-like illustration of the car on the left had a few squiggles on it. The one on the right, however, was almost completely colored in. How could that be? My brain could not absorb, register, and translate the image that my eyes saw.

We waited anxiously for the moment when Corey would be wheeled to the silent helicopter and safely shuttled to a hospital in Victoria. Once he received the necessary scan, we could then be assured that his condition was not serious. It was just a concussion. It *had* to be just a concussion. Suddenly, without warning, a flurry of activity erupted as the doors to the emergency room burst open. A still form on a stretcher wheeled past where we stood, and as I caught sight of Corey's bandaged head, I begged him to hold on. Tom asked that he be allowed to accompany Corey, but the doctor told him there was only room enough for the ambulance crew, a paramedic, and maybe a nurse. Perhaps his request wasn't heard correctly. He begged that he be granted permission to travel with our son. He promised to take up as little room as possible. "Just let me go with him," he pleaded. The doctor denied Tom's request. No choice did we have but to drive the 120-kilometer distance in our own vehicle. When I think back now, I am at a loss to say how we managed to drive all that way under our own steam. The closest I can come to offering an explanation is this: you do what you have to do for the people you love.

The night air held a crispness and a bone-numbing chill, but I barely noticed as we stood beside our car and stared transfixed at the helicopter. Jenn and Ally sat huddled in the backseat, too scared to move, too terrified to join us as we remained rooted to the ground, waiting for something to happen. Suddenly, the rotors began their sad, slow windup in preparation for liftoff. Time stood still as we waited in abject anticipation for its departure. When at long last it began its ascent, we spoke to Corey as if he stood beside us: "Hang in there, Corey, we're on our way." A broken promise to our son, a shattered pledge that we would stay with him no matter what, hung in the air as the helicopter sped off into the night. I silently asked him to forgive us. We watched the blinking red light of the helicopter fade as it melted into the black, empty night. The sound of the rotors dimmed, leaving a silence so heavy, I could feel it crushing my soul. I wondered how long it would take to arrive in Victoria. Minutes, I imagined, while we faced a journey of at least an hour and a half. Our poor son would be alone again, and it broke my heart.

As we left the city far behind, we encountered few vehicles along the way. Most travelers must have been at their final destination, waiting in joyful anticipation for the arrival of Christmas Day. The desolate highway stretched endlessly before us as Tom struggled to keep his mind focused on driving. Out of the seamless night, brilliant red Christmas lights appeared before us, high on a fence post—forming, of all things, the number seventy-three. When Tom saw them glowing in the night, he whispered, "Oh God, no." I didn't know what it meant but learned later that amateur radio operators, or ham operators, use this number when they sign off the air. It means good-bye. Both Tom and Corey were licensed as amateur radio operators.

We arrived at the hospital two hours later, bone weary and mind-numbed. Our daughters and I sank onto the cold black vinyl chairs in the waiting room while Tom sought out an official who was willing to answer his questions. The hospital had been informed that we were on our way, and now that we had arrived, the process of fixing up Corey could begin. *Good*, I thought. *The scan is done, so now we can get on with the next step of his recovery.* At long last, doctors and nurses would be able to help him, to stop the blood flow, to fix his broken bones. We barely had time to take the chill off those hard plastic chairs when once again, we were asked to please follow the person who spoke with Tom. We entered a low-lit, deafeningly quiet room. It felt like a room of death, a room safely sequestered from everyone so that weeping and wailing could not be heard beyond the walls. If we were going to be receiving good news, why were we in here? The door quietly closed as the lady left us with only our thoughts for company. What now? Was some sort of conference being conducted beyond the room where we sat? Was someone being informed that "the family" had finally arrived? Were the doctors trying to decide amongst themselves who would be the one to come in and "talk to the family"? How many times had they been placed in the unenviable position of having to break bad news to the family? Did they draw straws? Did they do the number game? Did one of them volunteer to talk to us? How did they decide?

My breath caught in my throat as the door cracked open, almost as if it wished it could stay closed. One look at the doctor's face and I knew; we all knew. We did not want to know. I wished I had some means of sealing this man's mouth shut so he could not utter the words I felt sure must be coming. I don't recall his exact words. I know the word "hopeless" was spoken. I know the phrase "Nothing we can do" spilled forth in the next instant. I looked at Jennifer as she clapped her hands over her ears to block out the awful truth. In response to the horror that this stranger spoke, she began to wail. I gazed at her and thought, *How could it possibly be that horrible? Is she picking up on something I am not?* Jennifer kept saying repeatedly, "You don't know what you're saying. You don't know Corey. You don't know him!" I felt as if I were an outside observer caught in a macabre game of "Who Done It." When next I glanced at the doctor, he was gone. Had he ever appeared? What had just happened here, and what did it mean? Tom opened the door and sought out someone who could direct us to the area where Corey was being kept. We were told that Corey was undergoing clean-up, and as soon as he was settled, we could see him. We each swam in our own thoughts in the deafening silence that followed, hardly aware that we had moved from the crying room to the waiting room outside the Intensive Care Unit. We waited—for what, I don't know. We sat and held hands. We breathed. We prayed. We waited in hopeless, paralyzing anguish.

When at last we were permitted to enter the cubicle where Corey lay, the doctor cautioned us to prepare ourselves as best we could. Corey's brain was swelling at an alarming rate, and nothing could be done to reverse the effect of the trauma he had suffered. I do not believe there is any amount of fortification parents can do beforehand to lessen the horror of seeing their child who is post-accident. My first reaction upon seeing Corey in the ICU was one of complete and utter disbelief. I could barely recognize him. This was Corey? He did not look at all like Corey. His face was swollen to the point that I felt for sure his skin would split open. His head remained bandaged, but all his clothing had been removed. A temperature probe was clipped to his left index finger. I found myself searching once again for that tiny scar I knew would be there. I felt for certain that they somehow got this person mixed up with Corey. His fingernails were blue, and there amongst all the wires, probes, and tubes was the little scar. I had no choice but to accept that the body lying before me was indeed the body of my son.

The only advice offered to us was to let him go in peace. Did that mean that the doctors, the so-called harbingers of health, were giving up on him? Letting him go in peace meant that we were being asked to allow him to die. How could Corey possibly die? He was fine eight hours ago. How did he go from being fine to dying? How? Why? The doctor told us they were unable to relieve the pressure building inside his skull; there were, however, drugs they could give him to ease the incredible pain he would be feeling. There was nothing else we could do. As a parent who has always been there to fix the hurt, ease the aches, kiss the bruises, soothe the fear, how was I expected to not *do* something? How does a parent simply stand by and let the unimaginable happen? How does a parent allow her child to die? Despite all my years and experience as a parent, I did not know the answer. I searched for something to do, anything. I felt so utterly and completely lost. Had I been able to find something to help Corey, something that the staff overlooked, I would have done it in a heartbeat, without question. Instead, once again, we sat, watched, and waited, for there was nothing else to be done.

Chapter Five

The Long, Lonely Vigil

Hope died a very hard death that night. Hope never wanted to be extinguished. Hope always wanted to believe.

No privacy was afforded us in that tiny open cubicle. People walking past could witness our lonely vigil. Time now stood still. The clock on the wall ticked away the seconds while the respirator clicked and sighed. We watched over our son. The overhead light was so bright, it almost hurt my eyes. I suppose it needed to be that way so the nurses could help Corey in whatever way remained. We talked to him, we touched him, and we tried to ease his troubled mind. He must have been so confused, wondering why he couldn't wake up. We tried to help him. The only way we knew to help was by talking to him. In the end, that was all that remained—we offered our voices to him in the hope that he would be able to draw whatever comfort he could from them. It became very important once again that he know we were there, and we were not going anywhere.

Nurses encouraged us to take a break, but we could not pull ourselves away knowing how precious time had become. Our poor girls, beyond the point of exhaustion, finally relented when I told them it was best if they tried to get some rest. I trembled, terrified by the pace at which events had unfolded but mystified that everything now seemed frozen in place. No matter how many times I closed my eyes, when I opened them again, we were not at home. We were in a brightly lit, sterile environment that was not my home. We awaited the arrival of death.

I dragged my weary body out to the waiting room. I helped the girls settle down. No blankets or pillows materialized to make them just a bit more comfortable. Instead, they lay on the cold imitation-leather sofas and closed their aching, tired eyes. They wanted to be in their own beds, away from this nightmare of a place. It didn't take them long to drift off to sleep, but my heart constricted when I thought of them waking up and realizing that this nightmare was true. Tom sat with me in the little crying room off the main waiting area and held my hand. I couldn't think of much beyond the fact that Corey lay alone in that bed. As we sat there, each lost in our own tortuous thoughts, Tom told me he would be returning to Corey's bedside. I couldn't join him; I was too frightened to move, too scared to have to face the reality of what was happening to our son, too paralyzed by fear to admit to myself that nothing I could do would help him. I stretched out on the little cot and prayed for something. I prayed for our family; I searched for an answer as to why we were here in this cold place so far from home; I talked to Corey. The anguish in my heart could not be borne. He was our first child, our only son, our future. He held in his hand all our hopes and dreams. How could God be so cruel as to take away our only son? How could He render us so powerless? What were the forces involved during such a crisis? Who made all the decisions? Who decided who lived and who died? Why did God decide that our son should die? Corey was so young, so innocent, and so vitally important to us. He was too young and too innocent to die. I searched for answers to questions I would never stop asking. I vowed I would never give up on Corey. I would not give up my fight to save him, for I believed he did not want to die.

I walked, I paced, and I talked to my son in the confines of that tiny room. I told him that just because I was not in the same room as him, it did not mean I stopped loving him. I felt weak, cowardly. I felt as if I had abandoned him. He needed to know I was right there.

Our all-night vigil began to take its toll on me. I lay down on the cot and silently asked Corey for permission to rest a while. Tiredness soaked through me. I begged that this place be banished from my sight. If I had the power to return home, this would become nothing more than a horrible nightmare. I drifted off to sleep and awoke with a terrifying start as the hydraulic door to the ICU opened. Was someone coming to get me, or did death enter the ICU? The clock on the wall read 4:00 a.m.

I felt I had been caught doing something bad. I slept as my child lay dying. Guilt and shame overcame me. In my dazed and confused state, I suddenly experienced an overwhelming need to speak to Corey. Time seemed to be running out. "Oh, Corey, I know you're scared. I know you don't understand any of this. But we are here. We always will be. But you cannot stay, Corey. You must be so scared and confused. You do not know what is going on. You were involved in a car accident, Corey, and you have been badly hurt. Your bones are broken, and you've got a real bad head injury. Your head must hurt so badly—it is so swollen. But you have to go, Cor. You can't stay here any longer. Corey, you have to go to the light. Uncle Dennis, Auntie Nita, and Auntie Micky are all there waiting for you. They will take good care of you, Cor. I cannot help you anymore, son. I am so sorry, but you are too badly damaged. You have to go, Cor. I don't want you to go, but you have to go. You can't come back to us. You will never be the same if you don't go. I'm your mother, and I know what's best for you. I would never do anything to hurt you, but you have to listen to me—listen to your mom. I love you, Corey, but I have to let you go. I don't want you to go. I love you, but I have to trust that this is best for you. Moms always know best, right? Please trust me, Corey." And with those words, I gave my son permission to die. I let him go. Why I spoke those words, I will never know.

At 4:20 a.m., Tom emerged from Corey's bedside to check on the rest of his family and deliver what we thought was good news. He told me that at 4:00 a.m., Corey started to emerge from his coma. He began to shake, and the nurse said, "Looks like he's starting to lighten up." Hope flooded through me as I realized he was going to be okay. The girls awakened and heard what had happened. Ecstatic, they immediately wanted to run to their brother and see for themselves this miracle of life returned. Before we could make our way to his side, a doctor approached us with the horrific news that she was seeking permission from us to harvest our son. Elation instantly metamorphosed into fear as her words fought their way into my brain. Harvest? Why would anyone want to harvest Corey if he was going to be okay? As soon as the girls heard those words, Jennifer began to scream and clutched her hands over her ears to shut out the doctor's awful words.

As I ran to comfort her, Tom led the doctor down the hall and quietly told her what he thought of her bedside manner. She displayed total disregard and an incredible lack of sensitivity toward us as a family. She left shortly afterward when she realized we would not be signing any forms for organ donation. We could not bear the thought of anyone removing our son's vital organs. We later learned that at 4:00 a.m., our son had suffered brain death. He went into crisis; his blood pressure soared, and his heart began a wild and frantic race. Tom sat beside him and talked him down. Only when Corey settled down did Tom dare leave his son's side and inform us of what had happened. Over the course of the next hour and a half, Corey's fragile condition began to deteriorate further.

We knew no hope remained, but in spite of that, we chose not to give up. Jennifer ran from the waiting room and bolted to her brother's side. We hung in there every last step of the way with Corey. We breathed for him, we watched over him, we agonized with him. We, above all else, wanted this nightmare to end. We wanted our boy to be safe and returned to the comfort of our home. We could not believe this had happened and was still happening. Comprehension became impossible. He was a gentle soul; why should he have to pay such a price? We paced, we watched, we waited. We were waiting for a miracle that never arrived.

Somewhere in the far-off distance, I heard the word *priest*. That word sent shock waves through my numbed mind, but somewhere it registered. The fight within began once again. There was only one reason for a priest to be called, and I was not prepared to accept the inevitable. I was not prepared to give up on my child. The thoughts inside my mind raged while I sat on the stool as if made of marble and observed all the activity around me. I felt completely detached from my body. I couldn't express my opinion, register any objection, or ask questions about what this person thought he was doing to my son. When the priest entered the cubicle, I wished with all my heart that this man of God would vanish. Who gave permission for this person, this priest to enter our lives and absolve Corey of his sins? I closed my eyes tightly as his words floated in the air. He walked around Corey's still form and muttered words about his soul being released from his body. I wondered where he had been given the authority to release anyone's soul from his body. I changed my tactic at that moment; I prayed with all my might that he would not succeed. I didn't want my son's soul to go anywhere. I forced my eyes open a crack and saw this complete stranger walk from one end of the bed to the other. He offered no consolation to us. We were nothing to him but an inconvenience. I knew then that, once again, all hope threatened to evaporate. I understood that when a person was given his last rites, it became the final plea to God to accept this person in heaven and forgive all his sins. These words were spoken when all hope was obliterated.

My son lay dying. Soon his soul would be released from his battered and broken body and sent . . . where? Was it in the room? What did his soul look like? I gazed around at all the monitors, the machines, the television screen suspended in the corner, the white-tiled ceiling, and yet I could not see anything that closely resembled a soul. After the priest made a hurried exit, silence filled the space where he had stood. Had it all been a dream? Things remained the same; Corey was still hooked up to the machines, his heart continued to beat, and we remained firmly cemented to the spot we had been in since that undeterminable hour in time. The priest hadn't killed him as I had feared. He may have given Corey permission to die, but my son did not comply. I felt as if I claimed a small victory. Just because he received the last rites did not mean Corey accepted them. My son and only my son would have the final say.

The scene before me refused to register, although I painfully acknowledged the presence of the monitors, tubes, hoses, and other hospital paraphernalia that all led back to the still form that lay on the bed. Ally sat between her dad and me as we watched this scene as if it were some terrible real-life drama. That's exactly what it was, wasn't it?

But the picture that remains with me to this day is the vision of Jennifer kneeling at her brother's bedside. The elevation of the bed to a comfortable height for the doctors and nurses meant that sitting in a chair left Jenn with her chin resting on the mattress. But the chair, another fine example of hard, naked, cold plastic furniture, provided the means for Corey's sister to minister to him when no one else would. On this unforgiving surface, she knelt. I doubt she felt the discomfort it caused her, so great was her attention on her brother. She held his hand tenderly as she methodically wiped the blood that continued to seep from the corner of his mouth. The respirator that breathed for him remained in place, yet somehow that blood found its way out.

My eyes kept track of the tiny animated heart that pulsated on the monitor over the bed. The numbers glowed brilliant green at me, changing from seventy-two to sixty-nine to over one hundred. I supposed this measured his heart rate. Other numbers continued to flash, and every once in a while a beep would be heard, as if the computer had to do a quick recalculation because the figures were changing too rapidly for it to keep pace. I realized later that these numbers represented his blood pressure.

Jenn never wavered in her new duty of closely monitoring all the equipment and maintaining her gaze on her brother's face. She felt it her personal responsibility to talk Corey out of this. It became her mission to save her brother, and she knew what needed to be done. She refused to leave his side, and she continued to wipe the blood that stubbornly pooled at the side of Corey's mouth. She talked to him as she watched the machines, wiping his face and never letting go of his hand. I listened as if swathed in cotton batting to the words, "That's it, Cor. You're doing it. That's it. You've got to keep that blood pressure up. That's it. Good job. Now watch your heart rate. It's slipping a bit. Come on, Corey; bring it back up a bit. That's the way." The numbers on the screen seemed to be changing with increasing rapidity, never staying the same or maintaining the same level for very long. What did normal blood pressure look like? The numbers flashed and danced too quickly. This could not be normal.

I laid my head on Tom's shoulder as I witnessed the incredible battle that played out before me. I knew in my heart that our child suffered. He would never give up, not for us or for himself. He did not want to die. He would not care about his own pain, but he would concern himself more with his sister's pain and her uncompromising faith in him. In short, he would never let her down. So he fought in the only way he had left. He listened to her and responded even though the doctor told us that there was no medical reason to believe he could hear or understand what she said. The power of love extended beyond normal bounds, and what we witnessed that day represented love in its most pure form.

Since the moment of Jenn's birth, she and Corey were two halves of a whole. As she knelt on that chair, she shifted her weight from time to time, but not once did she stand to take the pressure off her weary knees. She recited the same incantation with identical intonation over and over again. Some may say she acted selfishly, not wanting to do what was best for her brother. Some may say she fought a losing battle. Some may say she entered into direct combat with God. And some may say it was inevitable that God would win. God always wins. But Jenn willed herself to go the distance. She felt it her personal goal to save her brother from the evil clutches of death. She tried, and she fought right there beside him, literally shoulder to shoulder. They tried together to drive away the horror that threatened to consume our safe and secure family.

Each time those numbers on the screen increased even minutely, I rejoiced. But for every gain, there followed a loss. The figures began to fall in value, no longer able to recapture their previous highs. Our son was dying.

I remember leaving the area and walking with Tom as he struggled to determine the best course of action. We knew we faced a losing battle, and somewhere between the pacing of the hallway and the return to his bedside came the decision that perhaps we should donate his organs. It presented as a horrible thought to me, too awful for me to actually give voice to it. I could not fathom anyone ripping out my son's beating heart from his chest as it continued to pulse with life. I could not imagine his lungs removed from his body and given to someone else. I could not come to terms with anyone slicing open his body and removing those organs he needed to live. This would represent the ultimate in giving up. I would not be able to forgive myself for doing something so terrible to him.

And while we paced and tried to determine the right thing to do, another drama played out in the cubicle where Jenn and Corey remained. I did not witness it, but I wish I had. I heard about it days later as we tried to grasp the reality of what had happened in our lives. Like fog drifting in on a cold winter day, those words spoken to Jenn filtered through my frozen mind and were quickly swept away out to sea. But now, as I sit here trying to gather those words to my heart, I wish that I'd had the capacity to actually bear witness to the effect of such powerful sentences as they wielded incredible influence on a young girl's heart. That which was spoken to her would ultimately play a leading role in Jenn's destiny of becoming a registered nurse.

During the time of our absence, a nurse approached Jenn, gently extracted her from her brother's side, and said that she should take a break from the strain she was willingly placing upon herself. As the nurse gently led Jenn to the window, she said, "You know, we can't save them all. As much as we would like to do that, perhaps there is a higher power at work, and we are left feeling helpless against that power. As much as we would love to save everyone, it can't be done." I believe that with those words, the burden of responsibility for saving her brother's life was removed from Jenn's soul. She felt that somewhere deep inside, if anyone could have saved him, it could only be herself. Corey trusted her with his life, and she felt a responsibility to help him at a time when he needed that help the most. He remained powerless and defenseless in his struggle to fight against the dark curtain of death. All his precious energy went directly into listening to Jenn as she battled along with him. The ability to try to comprehend the enormity of the fact that his life, as he knew it, would soon be over would have been too overwhelming. He needed his sister.

When we returned to that room, we noticed a change in Jenn's tone and posture. We asked to speak to the doctor in charge of our son; we had made the decision that we would donate his organs. As we waited for the doctor's response, I noticed that the intensity of Jenn's voice as she spoke to her brother had changed. She no longer spoke with conviction and direction. She softened her voice as she told him he no longer had to fight. It was okay for him to rest. Her new role involved helping her beloved brother prepare to die. What an incredibly brave girl—she did what I could not do. I felt like such a coward in the face of such courageousness. I was not prepared to surrender my son to the unknown. But Jenn, with all the love she had for him in her heart and knowing full well how much this hurt her, decided to put her own pain aside and think only of Corey not struggling anymore. He would willingly continue this battle had Jennifer asked him.

How could a sixteen-year-old possess enough understanding, compassion, and courage to give another person who was so young, so full of life, such a vitally important part of her life, permission to die? It was more than I would ever have been able to do. My job was to protect them from harm, to keep them safe, and to make sure they remained happy. I failed miserably at keeping my son safe and free from harm. I could not accept that death would make him happy. However, in the end, we had no choice. Death would win.

Chapter Six

Make a Choice

As the new day finally dawned, and the first gentle strokes of light brushed softly across the sky, we found ourselves to be little more than empty, hollow shells. Doctors asked what our final decision involved. All hope abandoned, nothing left to do, Tom and I were led to a barren, impersonal examination room and asked to sit upon cold stainless-steel chairs. The doctor presented us with the results of his most recent assessment and told us our son was little more than a vegetable. Anger instantly flared as Tom informed him that Corey was a human being with two adoring siblings. As long as his heart continued to beat, he was a human being, not a vegetable.

I had never seen a professional become as contrite as that doctor did in that moment. He excused himself after we asked that he leave us while we summoned the courage necessary to face our children. We wearily plodded down the long hallway back to Jenn and Ally; we sat down heavily as we gathered them close to our hearts. They cried uncontrollably as we announced the results of the final series of tests conducted on Corey. The choice was now up to us. Would Corey live or would he die? It was simple—one choice or the other.

But I didn't want to make that decision. If God was going to take Corey, why didn't He just do it? He'd come this far without consulting with us. Why should the final word be ours? Who were we to decide? We loved this child too much to pass sentence and judgment upon him. Years invested in his upbringing, and for what? For this moment when we, his parents, would decide if he should live or die. Backed into a corner, we looked desperately for a way out. Attempts to reach

41

our family doctor proved futile. Relatives gave us the space they felt
we needed to do as we saw fit. In reality, we were not fit to be in
that hospital. It should never have come to this. Before we made our
final choice, we consulted one last time with the doctor. We needed
to know what to expect if we ordered the machines disconnected.
Chances were he would not breathe. Chances were that he would
die. Chances were that his heart would continue to beat, and when
it finally failed to receive the oxygen necessary as commanded by his
brain, it would cease its struggle to survive. This, the same heart that
began to beat days after conception, would stop, forever. What did
forever mean?

We entered the ICU for the last time. Our hearts heavy, our
minds deadened, we solemnly shuffled to where Corey lay. We
gathered around his bed for the last time. The lights were turned
down; all sense of urgency had long since vanished. Soft light gently
suffused his room, and for a moment, the institutional atmosphere
evaporated. The mood in that room was so peaceful, soft, quiet,
and incredibly sad. No violent winter storms raged outside nor did
brilliant sunshine flood into the room.

We asked that the medication and machines be shut down
simultaneously. God, this felt like we were witnesses at an execution.
A nurse entered and kindly turned off all the monitors. We would
not bear witness to Corey's faltering heart. At that moment, the
executioner made his entrance. He switched off the respirator, and
we heard the air escape in a rush from Corey's lungs. Was it possible
for the room to become even more silent? The respirator now turned
off, I focused my attention on my son, watching and praying in
futility that he would inhale. I held my breath as the air continued
its escape through his opened mouth. I waited and watched. He lay
motionless, so very still. He did not inhale. I took a breath and willed
him do the same. *Follow me, Cor. I will show you how it is done. If you
have forgotten, that's okay. I will help you learn. I will teach you!* He
remained still. Out of reflex, my breath caught, while Corey's didn't.

We knew what would come next as we placed our hands gently
upon his chest. We held his hand, we stroked his face, we told him
we loved him. We pledged to him that he would always be a member

of our family. But not once did we ask him to remain. We knew he didn't possess the power to grant our wish. He knew the options were stripped away, cast aside, and discarded. Time ceased to exist. A nurse finally entered and informed us, "Corey's heart has stopped beating." With that sentence, our lives ended too. We looked at him. We kissed him. We lovingly stroked the stubble that had started to grow upon his face. We knew we would have to leave, but our feet seemed glued to the tile floor. This seemed too cruel to be happening. The world as we knew it had stopped, yet everyone continued to move. No life remained in me, and the silent shell of Corey—the same body that twenty-four hours previously was lounging around the house, reading and refusing to go to work—lay silent and still. He no longer lived. As we began the motion of leaving, as if one, we turned at the same time for one last look and walked away. He was gone. "See you later, Cor."

I looked back one last time at Corey and told him I loved him. I glanced at the young nurse standing at her station. She sobbed heavily, tears streaming down her cheeks, and my heart went out to her. A complete stranger wept for us. I abhorred the idea that I would be leaving without him. What would happen next? What were we supposed to do? Make phone calls? Leave the hospital? Where would we go? How would we get there? How could this be happening? Corey was supposed to buy his truck, start his career as an electrician, find a girlfriend—but first and foremost, he was supposed to be home for Christmas. As Tom embraced me, forcing me away on feet made of cement, I begged Corey to follow. Yet he remained where he lay, silent and still. Neither my heart nor my brain could understand something like this happening so quickly. How could someone so young and vibrant go from unbelievably healthy and happy to a nonfunctioning, broken human being?

To this day, I fail to understand it. I gladly would have taken him in whatever state as a result of this horrible accident. All I wanted, all I wished was for him to be alive. All I wanted was for him to come home with us. The concept of souls and spirits remained too abstract and certainly didn't apply to our nineteen-year-old son. I felt pushed off a cliff without warning and, as I free-fell, I watched dispassionately as the ground loomed closer, rushing up to meet me. At that moment, I knew what it meant to no longer care about myself.

We returned to the waiting room outside the Intensive Care Unit as if pre-programmed. The surroundings looked unfamiliar, yet I recognized the clock and the phone on the table as I looked at them without really seeing them. A social worker joined us, bringing food to eat. I managed to swallow some soup, but it tasted artificial and lacked discernible flavor. I quickly set it aside. The sandwiches, leathery and cardboard-like, lacked appeal as well. The tea, barely lukewarm, sat untouched on my tray. I sustained myself while my son lay dead. I breathed and he could not. We sat in that room for an indeterminable length of time, unable to move, unwilling to take another step away. Beside us, smugly perched on a table, sat the black desk phone, taunting and mocking. Where were we to start? How were we to go about calling people and delivering news no one wanted to hear? Why were we handed that additional task as well? Wasn't playing God enough for one day? I felt sure that Tom's side of the family knew full well the extent of our crisis, but what about all our co-workers? What about my side of the family? The thought of repeatedly hearing the anguish in other people's voices coupled with the denial and disbelief that would surely follow made this more than I could bear. We sat in paralyzed fear while silently I begged for someone, anyone, to please rescue us. The only response I received was the silence that enveloped me, threatening to pull me under and never let me go.

Tom initiated our departure from the tiny, cramped room. One by one, we stood. My legs seemed incapable of holding my weight, and I sagged miserably against my husband. In my hand, I clasped a card from the hospital expressing sympathy. Inside, the name of the hotel where we would be staying marred the clean white surface. How that card came to be in my hand remains a mystery. Neither do I recall our exit from the hospital or the trip to the hotel. Did any one of us speak to another along the way?

When we arrived at the Empress Hotel, we stood in the foyer, waiting for our turn to check in. Two rooms in this posh hotel had been set aside for us to use as long as we wished. At the height of the Christmas season, this popular hotel kept two rooms available. Was our arrival expected? Had these rooms been booked long ago just for us, two days before Christmas? I gazed at the people who were dressed in holiday finery while we stood wearing the same clothes from the previous day. We must have presented a very strange sight—no luggage at our feet and no joy of the season present on our faces. Exhausted and numbed beyond the capacity it seemed possible for any human to endure, I wanted only a respite from the trauma I suffered. My head felt stuffed with cotton. I kept looking at my family and knew something was terribly wrong. Only four of us stood here. What about Corey? Why were we at this strange hotel when we should be at home preparing for Christmas? We should be getting ready for our annual drive to admire the Christmas lights around the city, making popcorn to snack on as we rode from place to place capturing as many sights as possible. Then we should be returning home because Santa Claus, who knew magically the exact moment we would arrive back home, would call our kids and speak to each of them. Would he call tonight and instead receive the recorded message on our answering machine? I didn't know; we wouldn't be there to take the call.

"Hello, Corey. This is Santa calling you. Corey, what do you want for Christmas this year?"

"My life."

We rode the elevator up to our rooms, located on the same floor but at opposite ends of the corridor. Jenn and Ally were adamant that we stay together, so we agreed to bunk as a family in one room. A bottle of sleeping pills mercifully materialized and required little coaxing to swallow and slip into oblivion. The girls bedded down on the fold-out sofa bed while Tom and I collapsed on the bed. Instantly, we fell asleep. I woke up dazed and confused and inexplicably glanced at the phone on the nightstand. The light flashed, indicating a message waited for us. I gently nudged Tom awake, telling him what I thought I might be seeing. Did anyone know where we were? How did they find us? When Tom called down, he found that my brother and his wife were in the lobby wanting to see us, but security denied them entry. How long had they been waiting? Tom asked to speak to Greg, granting him permission to come up, agreeing to meet them in the second unoccupied room. The kids lay sleeping. Before quietly slipping out of the room, I planted a gentle kiss on each tender forehead. I didn't want to risk them waking up and finding us gone.

They immediately woke up, begging us not to leave. We gave them as much reassurance as possible, promising to return as soon as we could. We entered the vacant room, and I noticed a vase of flowers and a card sitting on the bureau. Our first sympathy card delivered two days before Christmas, and I could only think of how it managed to find us so quickly. Was there an express sympathy-card counter open for business this close to Christmas? Flowers? In December? Food? Why? The first words I read about losing Corey to death, words designed to offer comfort, felt hollow and empty. I could not fathom him going to live with the Father of Us All. Why should he go live with someone else? We were his family. He belonged here with us. Anger instantly flared toward this Father of Us All. Who was he to suddenly decide that Corey was better off in His house and not ours? I dropped the card to the carpeted floor as if it was on fire.

Greg and Laura arrived shortly afterward, confusing me even further. Why were we in this hotel room in December talking about Corey as if he were dead? Why were they crying? Nothing made sense. We asked Greg if he and Laura would like to make use of the empty hotel room, and they accepted. We returned to our room a brief time later, immediately falling into a drugged sleep. I did not wake again until morning.

With the dawn came again the realization that Corey was not with us. As I opened my eyes and took in the strange surroundings, I began to remember. We were in Victoria, and the cold grip of reality tightened around my heart, squeezing so hard I could not breathe.

Slowly, one by one, we awoke, showered, and readied ourselves for the chore that lay ahead. We ordered juice and coffee; neither was touched. It seemed we had forgotten how to eat or drink. We made ourselves as presentable as possible, thinking we should go down to the dining room for some nourishment. As we sat at our table, the only thing to continually circle in my mind was that Corey was not with us. My eyes took in all the elaborate decorations; I could feel the sense of Christmas anticipation in the air, the staff so festively happy while Christmas carols played softly in the background. I closed my eyes in an effort to block it all out. I sat woodenly in my chair, ordered food I had no desire to eat, and tried to keep the tears at bay. My stomach felt as if a cold lead weight lived there as it cramped painfully in protest from lack of food and revulsion to eating. The lump in my throat continued to grow as I fought back emotions too numerous to identify. I dreaded facing what lay in wait upon our return to the room.

The kids busied themselves with packing up their meager belongings while Tom sat down heavily at the desk and extracted pen and paper from the drawer. He began to list everyone he would call and how he would break the news. People would not likely be at home for the holidays, so only the answering machines would pick up our call. I had neither the heart nor the stomach to leave a message like that on anyone's answering machine. When at last he picked up the receiver, he leaned heavily on the desk, voice breaking, as over and over again, he began with the same horrible sentence that drove the hurt in deeper and deeper each time he spoke: "I have some very bad news to tell you." I put my hands over my ears to block out the repetitive heartbreaking announcement. Each person expressed disbelief, repeating the same response over and over again: "Oh my God, not Corey!" Oh my God, it was true.

Tom called his sister who lived in Victoria; she insisted that we drive to her place before we returned home. I felt like socializing about as much as I felt like eating. We went anyway. Thus began the "pretend" era. Her house, decorated festively, the table set to perfection, and the children dressed in their Christmas best, seemed well orchestrated and meticulously choreographed. I felt I had walked into a theatrical performance. From the moment we entered her home, not a word, not an expression of sympathy, no condolences were offered. No one mentioned Corey or his absence. I sat like a statue, numb and cold, as I stared vacantly into space. Christmas cheer hung in the air, but my heart felt bleak and empty.

In all fairness, Tom's sister and her family only did what they thought best. I can imagine that before our arrival, everyone was given their cue on what to say—and, more importantly, what not to say. Christmas and death did not walk hand in hand. Perhaps they thought that if we witnessed firsthand the joyfulness and happiness, we would feel less miserable. Maybe they simply wanted to take our minds off our troubles. I obliged as best I could, pretending for the sake of the season. Pretending is such difficult work, but for the duration of our time in that house, I did exactly that. My thoughts continually drifted back to the hospital, and only when directly spoken to did I respond. I began to wonder if Corey had ever existed. Suddenly, I could feel myself beginning to suffocate. I could not wait to leave, to get away from this entire pretense, to return to the sanctity of our home. Only when everyone assembled before us as we prepared to leave did the grief that had been swelling like a balloon inside me burst forth. I actually apologized for breaking down and crying.

Less than twenty-four hours had passed since my son died, and instead of compassion, I received the suggestion that perhaps now was the time to seek out a competent therapist, someone trained specifically in dealing with a loss of this magnitude. Where did this desperate need to fix me, as if I were a broken toy, come from? I stood paralyzed as my sister-in-law told me that a modern medical professional would be able to perform the miracle of healing a broken spirit. My only requirement was a willingness to heal, to mend, and to get over this tragedy. She told me that given the gift of time, all would mend. I shook my head, trying to wordlessly convey to her that healing remained the furthest thing from my mind. The hurt penetrated too deeply to ever be consoled by words designed to heal.

I don't recall the trip home or entering the house when we arrived. Could this actually be the same place I had left less than forty-eight hours before, hurriedly packing and dashing off into the cold, dark night? I stood in the foyer and looked around me. The house remained as I had left it. I suddenly remembered the chicken I'd removed from the freezer just before I answered the phone. Where had I left it? I noticed flowers everywhere and, on the counter, a coiled newspaper carefully wrapped with yellow ribbon. It could only mean that the events detailing Corey's accident were contained somewhere within its confines. Were there any pictures? Not ready to open the newspaper but still needing to, I untied the ribbon and opened to the first page. Despair gripped me as I flipped to the second page.

Before my eyes was a picture of his car, unrecognizable, a twisted tangle of metal and glass. The photo, taken at night, lacked clarity. If two vehicles collided, then why did it look as if a van smashed into a tree? The back end of Corey's car, behind the driver's door, barely resembled a vehicle at all. I quietly refolded the paper and retied the ribbon, returning it to its place on the counter. My brain could not digest this black-and-white reality. I turned away from the kitchen counter, moving deftly, searching the house in vain. I wandered aimlessly from room to room, but I could not bring myself to go upstairs. Corey's room lay at the top of the stairs. I don't consciously know for what I searched, but my guess would be Corey. He was nowhere to be found. I placed my hand on the banister, grazing the garland that draped around it, and wearily plodded up, one step at a time. Once at the top, I glanced to the left, peeking into his room.

It remained just as he left it. Typical teenager's room—clothes scattered everywhere, towels tossed on the floor still damp from a shower two days before, computer equipment spread over every available surface waiting for repair, his closet bulging with electronic gear and gadgets. I stepped carefully over the towels and sat on his bed. I waited, but no tears came. Disappointment seeped into my pores. If he really died, how come I could not feel his presence? Why were things not floating around in midair? Do people when they die really just expire and cease to exist? Did nothing remain when they died? Where was the heart of Corey? Where was he? If any sort of connection existed between me and my child, how come I could no longer feel him?

If possible, that room became quieter than when I entered. Despondently, I went back downstairs feeling worse than when I went up. I removed Corey's graduation picture from the living room and brought it into the dining room. I found Tom gazing sightlessly out the window, his reflection in the glass painted with anguish and despair. I approached him, gathering his body close to mine. He turned as we clung to one another tightly, our vision filled with the sight of Corey's picture. Tears fell . . . and then suddenly, without warning, something happened. My jaw dropped as we both said, simultaneously, "Can you feel that?" I felt something, maybe Corey, enter my body, filling me with tingly warmth almost like warm chills.

I am ashamed to say my memory of the rest of that night remains unclear. Nightfall arrived, and I can remember Jenn's boyfriend, Carlos, appearing at the door. I recall her mad dash down the stairs as she raced to answer the door, grabbed his hand, and pulled him upstairs. Carlos looked confused, completely taken aback by the force with which Jenn dragged him away. Exhausted and beaten, Tom and I retreated to the safety of our bedroom.

Jarred awake suddenly the next morning by the ringing of the telephone, I awoke dazed and confused. Upon opening my eyes, the horror of the past two days seemed nothing more than a bad dream. Back at home, safe in our bed, I held onto those thoughts as tightly as I could. My life broke apart again when Tom said the call was for me. It took five little words to shatter the bubble that protected my fragile mental state: "Karen, I am so sorry." I gaped at Tom and knew this reality wasn't a bad dream after all. Christmas morning had arrived, and Corey was gone. I talked on the phone while Tom slipped downstairs to make coffee.

When he returned with two steaming mugs of freshly brewed coffee, Tom said he wanted to tell me something. We snuggled in bed and, as gently as he could, he told me about the visit he had received from Corey the night before.

Tom said he slept heavily but instantly awakened when the door to our bedroom opened. He stared transfixed as Corey stood in the entrance to our room. Tom felt overcome by an incredible sensation as something tried to push its way into his body. Panic-stricken, he fought back, and the feeling immediately receded. He knew there would be a second attempt and prepared himself as best he could. The force, stronger than before, was accompanied by Corey's voice imploring his father, "Dad, I just want to give my mom one last hug." Immediately, Tom relaxed and welcomed Corey, wrapping his arms around me gently, squeezing me and hugging me. The moment Corey completed his mission, the presence left Tom's body. Depleted of energy and exhausted beyond belief, Tom collapsed and instantly fell asleep.

I could not believe his good fortune. I could not believe he thought it a dream. But mostly, I could not believe I missed my son's hug. I gathered my arms around my body, mimicking the embrace, and squeezed tightly. How hard had he pressed Tom's body to mine?

The day—dull, grey, and rainy—did nothing for my battered spirit. Our Christmas tree stood proudly in the center of the living room, surrounded by a few presents. Santa had forgotten to visit our home. Nestled next to the tree lay the project I'd asked Corey repeatedly to clean up. The wires, tools, and bits and pieces all were as he left them. I felt my heart breaking apart, as painful contractions threatened to engulf me. What did I do that day? Did I get dressed? Did I eat? Did my family eat? Did anyone come over or call? The weather and the utter and complete feeling of loss are the only things I recall with clarity.

Chapter Seven

The Exchange of Gifts

Christmas Day was dismal and bone-chillingly cold. Rain poured outside as fiercely as the pain flooded my heart. How long before the grief overflowed my banks?

Ours is a very temperate climate on Vancouver Island and as such, it has always rained on Christmas Day. But that year as the temperature dropped, it began to snow with a vengeance, accumulating on the ground and clinging to the trees within moments. As day blended into night, we watched outside our window as the snow continued to cascade from the heavens. I waited, expecting at any moment to hear Corey call out to Ally, "Hey, Al. Let's go see where else it's snowing." I wished to hear them climb into his car and take off, tires crunching and biting into the freshly fallen whiteness. It didn't happen. This snow, this small miracle seemed a gift from Corey, designed to comfort and assure us that he remained close. For the briefest of times, the world became a magical and wonderful place made possible by the bond of love we shared with Corey. That day gave birth to a new era where belief became the foundation and faith surrounded it, reinforced with the greatest love of all. Without question, the power of Corey was hard at work.

Christmas Day felt like a day of mourning. The joyous anticipation, the warm family times, the delicious smell of dinner cooking in the oven, were all absent that day. People dropped by to see us later that evening. No Christmas greeting at the door, no happy faces, no presents opened and tucked beneath the tree. Everywhere I turned, my eyes met pain and anguish, disbelief and horror. Tears kept clouding my vision. All I truly wanted was the peaceful state of deep, dreamless sleep, my haven where pain would stop and dealing with this new forced reality could cease. I welcomed the opportunity to rest as readily as a person thirsted for water on a hot summer day. I readily relinquished the reins of sorrow to another invisible driver. I wondered how I would ever cope.

With Christmas Day over, the endless stream of phone calls and people entering our home increased. A tragedy of this magnitude meant word would quickly spread, faster than a wildfire on dry, parched landscape. Cards and flowers flowed in steadily each time the doorbell rang. I moved around completely numbed, unable to comprehend as I walked from one room to the next, shell-shocked, dazed, and disoriented.

One day bled into the next, and while I drowned in grief, Tom assumed control over the details of Corey's funeral. He alone chose our son's coffin, a task no father should have to do for his son. He contacted the funeral home and arranged for the transfer of Corey's body back home. I recall someone recommending a funeral home, but as soon as I heard those words, I mentally shut down. Tom oversaw so many details while I stayed home and talked to whoever happened to stumble across my path, offering a sympathetic ear. I suppose I dealt with my tragedy in the only way I knew. I wanted to insulate myself from reality rather than participate. Nothing made sense to me, and no matter who I spoke to, no one could help me put things into perspective. I heard the words "Poor Karen," but even that phrase failed to fully register the true meaning of everything that revolved around me.

Sooner or later, my self-imposed state of denial would end, and I would need to deal with Corey's impending funeral service. It happened much sooner than I anticipated. When Tom mentioned that he needed my help, I angrily lashed out—I did not want to help anyone with burying my son forever. Someone witnessed this outburst, pulled me aside, and as gently as possible reminded me that Tom had handled all these details on his own. The time to drag myself out of my cocoon and offer a voice in my son's final arrangements had arrived.

I felt inadequate when asked to aid in preparations for the funeral of my child. Tom introduced me to Peggy, who had assumed responsibility for overseeing all the events at the church. I instantly developed a strong dislike for her, not because of the person she was but rather her way of presenting herself. She bravely faced me, quite aware of my open hostility, and gently admitted her lack of knowledge when it came to choosing music for the funeral of a young person. That statement instantly hit home. Corey was too young for something designed for old people. Funerals were for people who had lived a full life, people who gave up on life, people with worn-out and tired bodies. Funerals were not designed for vibrant young people. A funeral was not for Corey. Yet it would happen, regardless of my resistance. She asked me which songs I wanted to include. I wondered why she thought I possessed the necessary capacity to make an informed decision. I pushed back the hostility growing in my brain long enough to say I would not tolerate organ music. I felt the softness of piano better suited the occasion, much gentler than the piercing voice of the organ.

The first song we chose was "The Rose" made famous by Bette Midler. Peggy knew a young lady who would sing this song for Corey to perfection. We continued to work together, and I realized this service would be our final gift to Corey. As a result, I immediately developed little tolerance for anything that was less than perfect, quite a contrast from my disinterest of a few hours before. I chose the remaining songs with relative ease as the pieces of the puzzle effortlessly fell into place. His service would end with a song by Enigma, "Return to Innocence," the same song he was listening to when his life ended, the last song he ever heard. Within fifteen minutes, we were finished.

Things quickly fell into place, but only because Tom and I became very particular about the way things should be handled. Then a glitch happened. The warm, inviting room upstairs in the church where we hoped to hold the reception had been previously booked and was therefore unavailable. Although I was assured that everything would be done to secure it for our purpose, an alternative needed to be found just in case. At the end of a long hallway, down a longer flight of stairs, and through another cold hallway lay option number two: the gymnasium. As I stood in the doorway, the emptiness and desolation of the enormous room struck me full force. Corey could not be honored here. He always hated the cold. I was told once the tables were set up, the heat was turned on, and the empty space was filled with people, it would be warm and inviting. I remained skeptical. As we turned away and walked back upstairs, I reiterated that every effort should be made to reserve the warm room upstairs. The gymnasium felt too much like a grave.

The sequence of events leading up to Corey's funeral remains a blur. I know an extraordinary number of people surrounded me. Plenty of food was laid out throughout the house, an endless buzz of conversation constantly filled the air, and someone always seemed ready to embrace me. As I threaded my way through the maze of people and all their emotions, I found a vast emptiness where Corey once stood. I walked and searched the house many times over, never finding what I sought.

Tom and I held Corey's service on December 30, 1994. The night before, we hosted a service of farewell for anyone who wished to visit Corey one last time. That night, I would see my son for the first time since he died.

As I entered the church lobby, the funeral director came forward to greet me. He asked if I would like to go up and see Corey. My first impression of the man did not flatter him—he seemed anxious, pushy, and unnaturally proud. I hesitated. Fear and anxiety overwhelmed me; seeing Corey would force me to face an awful truth. I asked for a moment to adjust. From where I stood in the foyer, I could see his casket. I knew he was there. Instantly, the hesitation I experienced vanished as I felt myself drawn to him, mesmerized by the thought that an opportunity lay before me to feast my eyes upon my son. I cautiously approached, afraid I would awaken him. He lay there so silent and still. His chest did not move. His body seemed as hard and unforgiving as alabaster. His closed eyes did not flinch; I noticed his left eye returned to color, no longer black and blue. The skillful hand of the undertaker applied artificial color to his face, adding an unnatural rosiness to his pallor.

I gazed at him in awe, struck by his youthfulness. His hands lay folded across his stomach, his fingernails no longer blue. I touched him; there was no life or warmth lingering in that cold unyielding body. His life force had fled. I continued to look at him, spellbound. I willed him to get up, to quit playing such cruel games. I silently implored him, "Please, don't do this to me, to us. Come back, please just come back." He remained silent and still.

The next day, when I entered the church for the funeral service, I instinctively stepped back, overwhelmed by the number of people in the lobby. Far off in the corner, I spied the collage we'd constructed of Corey's short life. Days before, we'd sifted through countless pictures of Corey and our family, moments captured in time. Included with the photos was the outfit he wore when we brought him home from the hospital on November 30, 1975. Displayed next to his infant sleeper was his first baseball cap and, finally, his last cap. I pressed through the crowd with only one goal in mind: I needed to be near Corey again.

As I forged a path through the seemingly impossible blockage, I caught sight of Iris. She and Corey had worked together at the same electrical firm, forming an unusual and special bond. She doted on Corey as if he were her grandchild. He, in turn, helped her out in whatever way he could. She admitted to Tom years before that she preferred to avoid funerals at any cost. Yet here she stood, present at Corey's service. Tom and I slipped into the back room to see Corey one more time, and again, I prayed with all my might that he would get up and end this nightmare. Still, he did not move. I tried so hard to impress upon him the urgency of the matter; time was running out. Soon, he would be locked away forever, and there would no longer be any chance to escape this nightmare.

When the moment arrived for the lid of the coffin to be lowered, I could barely stand it. Corey would be taken away from me, this time for good. With the closing of the casket, only one thought remained in my mind. I wanted to crawl inside and hold him close for all eternity. I felt Tom reach for me while the girls placed their hands on my shoulders as if they could read my mind. The lid softly closed, and I watched as the fasteners were locked in place. Time slowed to a dreadful, painful crawl.

I was jolted from my reverie when Tom told me the time had arrived for the service to begin. People rose to their feet as we entered, Corey leading the way as always, blazing a trail for us to follow. When we stopped, my hand reached for his casket and lingered. I was forced to let go to take my seat. I uttered not a sound throughout that whole service. My heart broke time and time again. My eyes remained glued to where he lay, for I could not look away. Atop his casket, we placed a yellow silk rose given to us by our neighbor. Corey loved yellow roses. I don't know how Harriet knew this.

The service remains a blur for me. I recall parts and pieces, the eulogy, the music, the singing, but everything else is lost. Toward the end, the young lady began to sing "The Rose," and I felt myself drawn to my feet. I placed my hand on the casket as if checking for a heartbeat. Tom instantly appeared at my side, followed quickly by our daughters. We bowed our heads while holding hands. Jennifer's boyfriend joined us, then Corey's friend Christopher came up. We wept. I raised my tear-stained face to watch in amazement as the whole audience rose to their feet, making their way to where we stood. Before long, a complete circle of love surrounded Corey. The spontaneity of the moment lent it power. Could Corey feel the love exuding from everyone who came to honor him? All too soon, the song ended, and people returned to their seats. The end of the service rapidly approached. Corey would leave our lives soon, this time forever, and I was not prepared for that. I could not imagine never seeing him again. I could not grasp the concept of forever. I didn't know what that meant.

The pallbearers assumed their places, preparing to carry Corey away. At that precise moment, "Return to Innocence" began to play. I didn't think my heart could break again. At this rate, I wouldn't recognize my own heart. How long could a broken heart continue to beat? Music filled the church, swelling to the rafters, haunting me with its melody.

As they placed Corey's casket in the hearse, I prayed for all I was worth that this would not continue. The procession moved toward that final moment of departure. We had decided to cremate Corey, but Tom felt he needed a symbolic sprinkling of dirt on the casket. The four of us pitched a handful of dirt on his coffin; no other volunteers came forward. The minister presented to each of us a framed picture of Corey along with a poem written by Tom's hand but inspired by Corey. I clutched my gift close to my chest. The minister gave Tom the crucifix propped inside the casket. When the doors to the hearse slammed shut in preparation for departure, I began to shiver uncontrollably, but not from the cold.

As the engine started and the van began to pull away, I tried one more prayer. The van kept driving away. I watched for as long as I could. When it slipped out of sight, I continued to stare at the spot where last I had seen it. If not for someone dragging me away, I would be standing there today.

Despite my protests, we held the reception in the gymnasium—but in the end, it didn't matter. We entered the formidable room, and Tom vanished from my side. I stood firmly mortared to the spot at which he left me. People drifted near me and then faded away. Someone brought me something to eat, for how else had this food and cup of tea appeared in my hand? People hugged me and cried on my shoulder. I comforted them. I could do nothing else. I was numb, devoid of feeling. I remember noticing all the plants we had received for Corey's memorial garden in a far-off corner of the gymnasium. They looked so tiny in all that space, looking as lost as I felt.

An entourage of people followed us home, filling our home with laughter and conversation. Company was perhaps the best thing for me. It kept my mind occupied and prevented me from having to face another moment without Corey. But the realization that if not for his dying, all these people would not be here, made it a double-edged sword, a reminder as well as a distraction. The hour grew late as people slowly prepared to leave and return to their own normal lives. How I envied them.

The suggestion of counseling surfaced again, and in my hand, I held material on grief management and names of support groups. My foggy brain could not fathom the depth of such things. We'd never needed counseling or support before; why would we need it now? What in the world was happening? All the love and support I needed filled my home with all these friends and relatives. Despite the fact that I had been plunged into a cold ocean of fear and death only six days before, I knew what I needed. I needed people who cared about us. I needed warmth and love from everyone who professed to so deeply care for us. Little did I know that the love and support so generously offered came with an expiration date, forcing me to face my naïveté in believing that we were not alone in this thing.

As people slowly began to trickle out the door, they professed a desire to stay but knew they needed to be on their way. After everyone left, I was beginning to tidy things up when suddenly Jenn appeared from nowhere, telling me she needed to speak to her dad and me. She was holding up surprisingly well, and I wondered where she managed to find such resolve. I stopped and gave her my undivided attention. I clearly saw the battle raging below the surface as Jenn struggled to find the right words.

"I was in the bathroom brushing my teeth, when suddenly I was no longer there. As I gazed in the mirror, I left my body and went to some point in the future. There before me lay the reason for Corey's death. After I was given this insight, I went back to my body and there I was as I had been, standing in front of the mirror, brushing my teeth."

Jenn is a very pragmatic person, but the driving need to seek the reason behind her brother's death consumed her. She *had* to know and would not rest. After she finished her story, I began to pummel her with questions. Where did she go? What was the future like? But most importantly, what was the reason? She looked at me with woefully sad eyes and replied, "I can't remember." I knew she felt bad. Yet this knowledge managed to sustain her, and for that I was grateful.

New Year's Eve dawned bright and clear. The snowfall was a distant memory and only the occasional bank of snow could be found cuddling the curb by the roadside. The wind howled in agony, giving the outside air a crisp freshness. As I peeked out the front door, I noticed that our outside Christmas lights were on. Controlled by a photocell, they normally cycled off as soon as the sun made its appearance. Instead, they brightly shone in the blazing sunshine. As I puzzled over this strange event, suddenly they turned off.

"Well, so much for reading something into this," I thought. I began to search everywhere for signs that my child still remained here, not far from home. I believed his spirit lingered, but I needed proof. I knew that if he needed to make us aware of his presence, he would work whatever miracles were available to him. As if on cue, the Christmas lights burst back to life, brightly burning in the glaring sunshine. Ever the skeptic, yet needing to know, I reached for the light switch and held my breath as I flipped it off. The lights did not flicker. I snapped the switch back on. They continued to glow. Throughout the rest of the day, they blinked on and off at irregular intervals. Was this some sort of Morse code?

A few people came over to see us as day gave way to evening, and 1994 prepared its departure. They came to help see us through to the next year. After suffering the silence of an empty home on my own for a few hours, I was ready for company again. I needed to talk about Corey again and again. *Need* is such an inadequate word. I burned and yearned to talk to anyone who would listen. It didn't take long to realize that my constant chattering was neither appreciated nor warmly received. I swallowed back the hurt and pretended all was well. It was, after all, more important for everyone to feel comfortable.

After we ushered in the New Year, my false bravado began to crack, the wilting of my spirit evident to all. We escorted our friends and family out the door, and their departures were uneventful except for one. Jenn's boyfriend, Carlos, one of the last people to leave, walked out to his car, which sat parked on the road in front of our house. After saying goodnight, Jenn stood outside to watch him go.

As he made the move to get into his car, the headlights and taillights suddenly came to life, flashing in unison. Carlos stepped away from the car and looked toward Jenn. She raised her hands and mouthed the word, "What?" He answered with a shrug of his shoulders, as bewildered as Jenn. As suddenly as the spontaneous lighting display started, it stopped. It could only mean one thing—Corey was hard at work, letting us know that he was still around. Carlos got into the car, started the engine, turned on the headlights, and drove off into the velvet black night without further incident.

I envied everyone the relative ease they had returning to their own lives. I wish the same could be said for me. By New Year's Day, the phone had ceased to ring. People believed we needed to be left alone. We did receive ongoing support from a niece who so kindly gave of her time. She was a welcome link to reality and life, exactly what I craved. Imagine my shock when she told me she'd received a warning to back off. She was told that if she didn't, we would never learn to stand on our own. Outsiders should not be there for us to lean on and depend on too heavily, as it was not healthy.

This advice went directly contrary to everything that I believed. I wondered how leaning on another could be called unhealthy. For instance, if I leaned on someone and they in turn leaned back on me, didn't we then form some resemblance to standing upright? Without support, I simply fell over, unable to right myself. I thought that when tragedy struck, family remained the one true element that could be counted on. Friends might abandon us, but family stuck like glue—they would stand by our side no matter what. People caught in the emotional turmoil of sudden death required love and strength as fortification to get from one moment to the next with the hope that someday they might be able to cope with the bigger equation of handling one whole day and then another. Total abandonment seemed unthinkable. Death could not divide and conquer that which stood tall and true. I watched as, one by one, the pillars of support around me crumbled and fell away. I needed, above all else, someone to simply listen to me. I needed to purge myself of all these awful feelings. I needed someone to listen and not pass judgment. I needed a compassionate ear, and it deeply saddened me when I found out, however innocuously, that this could not be good for me.

Out of courtesy to Ally, we held Christmas on the second of January. She couldn't understand why her presents sat unopened after all the time that had passed since Christmas morning. We agreed, but this meant we would have to face another unpleasant task. What were we to do with Corey's presents? Should we return them or keep them wrapped? Tom said Corey needed to see what he received for Christmas. So with heavy hearts, we opened his gifts for him and laid them out on the carpet in full view, gifts which my brother Greg and sister-in-law Laura spent hours wrapping in the days before Corey's funeral. We snapped pictures; we admired all that Ally received. At the end of this most taxing challenge, we cried. Thoughts of how unfairly life treated us, how Corey should be here to do this himself, compared nothing to the realization that these gifts would never be used.

A few days later, Tom's boss paid us a visit. Rob owned a condo on a local ski hill and thought perhaps we could use an excuse to escape life for a while. He kindly offered its use for a few days. We didn't ski, but the offer of getting away from the claustrophobic confines of the house was greatly appreciated. During the time Rob spent at our house, he mentioned something strange that had happened down at the waterfront.

In October, Corey had constructed a Christmas tree for the local port authority. It was made of steel tubing to which he had attached Christmas lights. This structure was then fastened to the top of a pole only accessible by extension ladder. The tree measured sixty feet in height and thirty feet wide at the base, a visible beacon to boats travelling in the Strait of Georgia. Rob told us that in the middle of this steel tree, a complete circle of light bulbs had burned out. The lights on the perimeter all functioned, and it seemed odd to him that this happened. He said it was as if something had gone through the middle, causing a power surge to burn out the Christmas bulbs. I wanted so desperately to see this for myself, but I couldn't do it. I feared it could be true, that the power of Corey's soul would be capable of causing lights to fail.

It's not that I doubted these paranormal events, but neither did I wish to seek reasons and explanations as to why all these things happened so soon after Corey's death. Perhaps I wanted to believe that my son wished to communicate with me. However, given that the spirit of Corey chose to deal with a human being, one born with limitations, he proceeded with caution. Too much evidence would be overwhelming, thus creating fear. So instead, I received small miracles in minute doses. They became firm anchors that, when linked to other small miracles, began to form a chain. That chain ultimately joined me to Corey. All else severed, I didn't wish to cast aside the lifeline he creatively constructed for me. This became my way of coping when life overwhelmed me.

Chapter Eight

Reality Check

It's difficult to discover ways to occupy your time when energy levels are low. But I tried to busy myself in any way I could. After all, that was one of the first pieces of advice I received. Good advice, perhaps, but when one's world has been knocked about and shattered, sometimes the simple act of breathing is more than one can manage. In an effort to divert my attention toward something more constructive, Tom and I assumed an active role in the investigation of the deadly accident that cost Corey his life. If not for a comment from an insurance adjuster, we likely would have taken what the police said as gospel and left it at that. But we were told speed was definitely a factor, and a collision of this magnitude could not have happened at fifty kilometers an hour. The driver of the van, who sustained minor injuries, was clearly at fault but without solid proof of drunkenness or substance abuse, there was little we could do to elevate the charges from driving without due care and attention to anything that would reflect the death and destruction he caused.

We attempted to find out from the police what transpired on that fateful day and what we could expect in the final analysis. The police, hesitant to share their findings, left us little choice, so we hired an engineer to help us understand how an accident of this magnitude could happen on a quiet residential street. We coordinated all the incoming information while we wearily plodded on.

In the end, after countless hours of consultation and thousands of dollars we could ill-afford to spend, we learned nothing other than to reinforce the fact that the legal system had little to do with justice.

Prior to Corey's death, I worked as a secretary. I loved my work as much as I loved the people. I felt like an integral part of a very large and caring family. Everything changed when Corey died. I found I couldn't immediately return to work. I knew I needed time to regain my footing, but when asked how much time I needed, I came up blank. Time, often distorted, felt compressed. It became difficult to distinguish one moment from the next. Regardless, things continued to change. Sympathy cards in the mail slowed to a trickle. Invitations to dinner, nights of card playing, anything to take my mind off my sorrow, even briefly, I welcomed. I clearly recall the day those contacts ceased.

On the morning of what I call the *day of change*, Tom and I both awakened at the same time. While sipping coffee in bed, we realized we felt completely lost. No plans for the day cluttered the calendar, and both of our daughters were at school. I could not figure out why I felt so blue, and as the day endlessly stretched before me, the feeling intensified. We ran a few errands together, but always the sadness lurked at the edge. The deep pain would not let up no matter how hard I tried to find ways of easing it. Only at the end of the day when I turned to Tom did I realize that it had been exactly one month since Corey died—a month that felt like a lifetime. Once I identified the reason for my deep despair, I embraced and accepted the penetrating sadness that permeated my soul. If allowed to talk about my deep hurt to anyone, I probably would have pinpointed it much sooner. But I found that things took longer to figure out when forced to do them on my own, especially when grief and pain clouded my thinking and judgment.

From that moment on, I admitted that Tom and I were forgotten by friends and family alike. I felt as if I too had died. Everyone returned to their own lives, and I felt as if I no longer mattered. I questioned why this happened. I turned inward and felt this meant I handled something poorly. Was I punishing myself? I tried to reach out to others, to let them know I needed them, but those attempts were

Karen Frenette

always met with a condescending air. Calls kept brief and to-the-point didn't allow much time for soothing. As I was not encouraged to express my sorrow and feelings, it became more evident that I was on my own. Tom returned to work by the end of January; physical labor served him well. He clearly required an outlet for his pent-up emotions. I began to write in my journal on a daily basis.

One night, we received an invitation to Tom's sister's house for dinner. Pinned to her wall was a copy of Corey's obituary. I gazed at it, mesmerized, and began to read it over. Totally engrossed in what I read, I paid little attention to the conversation going on around me. She looked up from washing dishes and told me, "Don't be reading that sad thing." Out of respect for her, I stopped. I felt guilty, caught doing something unforgivable. On a subsequent visit to her house, I saw that the death notice had been whisked away and banished from their lives forever. If it was out of sight, did that remove it from her mind as well? Was it supposed to be removed from mine too?

When we did visit with relatives, we were always asked if we were attending grief-therapy sessions. No longer veiled or disguised, the so-called *helpful* suggestions became more vocal and insistent. In fact, on the rare occasion when the phone did ring, counseling and therapy were always mentioned. It would be years before we found that the people best trained to help parents such as ourselves were other parents who had walked the same difficult path. Therapists listen, as that is how they earn a living. They guide people through the expected, predictable cycles and swings of emotion caused by grief. They can't say for certain how long these cycles and swings last or even when to expect them. Each person experiences grief differently, making it very individual and unpredictable. But relatives did offer the vague reassurance that somehow this journey of grief would become easier with time. Did time hold a giant eraser gripped tightly in its fist, ready and poised to rub out the existence of my child?

People told me I should return to work. They felt I needed to occupy my thoughts with other things instead of obsessing over my son's death. Out of desperation, I made a valiant attempt to go back to my job. This good plan deemed vital to the state of my mental health lasted two and a half hours, a complete waste of time. Co-workers

66

seemed very anxious that I recover, that I magically rebound to wholeness and wellness. When someone dared tell me I was healing nicely, I crumbled under the weight of those words. My anger flared, and I wondered who she was to judge me like that.

I tried to talk to the people I thought were my friends. With all my questions brushed off like lint, I searched in vain for validation that death did not end the life of a soul. They told me I imagined things. They told me I was under a great deal of stress and prone to making mountains out of molehills. Yet no one actually took the time to find out what I really felt on the inside. I was judged solely on how I appeared on the outside.

I have always valued the happiness that walks hand in hand with memorable occasions like birthdays and anniversaries. A true romantic at heart, I would go to extraordinary lengths for those I loved. I never realized until Valentine's Day arrived how much I missed my old life. Tom had to attend a course in Vancouver and would be gone for Valentine's Day. I felt terribly blue and horribly unhappy. I called up my niece, begging her to stay with the kids and me. I needed company, someone to help me maintain my sanity. I knew this was an awful lot to ask of a person; she had a husband and a life of her own. But she assured me that it wouldn't be a problem. Her husband completely understood. She stayed overnight but left the next day. I gave her my word that I would be okay. It seemed I needed emotional support, just not twenty-four hours a day.

I began to formulate a plan involving the creation of a Valentine's cake. The thought of Tom returning home that night buoyed my spirits to the heavens. The day before, I would not have been able to even contemplate taking on such a monumental task. Yet I would produce this cake from scratch and spend hours decorating it. Corey stood beside me, helping me complete what my heart sought to do.

Suddenly and without warning, disaster struck. Ally decided to sample my cake and in the process, I felt she caused irreparable damage. I unleashed the full brunt of my anger on her. She immediately raced up the stairs and fled to the safety of her room. I lost control; I said hurtful things, and nothing I could say or do would ease the painful sting of my words. All this anguish because her childlike innocence compelled her to merely sample. After all, how could I blame her? When was the last time I had baked anything? The phone rang during this tirade, and my sister-in-law was quite alarmed at my high state of anxiety. I explained about the ruined cake, but she could not understand what caused me to become so unglued. I know she regretted phoning as surely as I regretted being caught having a bad moment.

These bad moments did not always make for a completely bad day; like a storm, they passed over and blew away. They were nothing more than parts and portions of the complete picture. I lost the ability to make any type of rational decision, the capacity to experience a good moment or suffer through a bad one. I became a prisoner of time held hostage by grief.

When Tom called later that night asking if I could pick him up, he wasn't afraid or puzzled by my distress. He completely understood and assured me that Ally's intentions were not wicked or spiteful. She acted like the thirteen-year-old child she was, just as mischievous as her brother and sister had been at that age. I think it would have been easier to deal with something like a ruined cake if I were allowed to cry for Corey, rage for him, scream at the injustices of life when I needed to instead of when it was convenient for everyone else. It was never acceptable, so I learned to keep it to myself.

The month of February also became the month we dealt with Corey's room. Many weeks had passed since his death, and it would have been easier to just let his room become a living memorial, somewhere safe to go, to remember and think about him. But practicality pushed its way to the surface. His room could be put to better use. So that left the question: how can a parent best prepare herself to actually begin formulating a plan to tackle such a heavy burden? What was to be done with a room filled with a lifetime of precious possessions—stuffed animals, clothes, compact discs, magazines, comic books, electronic gadgets and computers left in various stages of disrepair, electronics that waited patiently for the return of the magician who would miraculously restore them to fully functioning and valued machines? What would I do with the mountains of memories, and perhaps more importantly, why should I have to do anything with them at all?

How was I to put my heart aside long enough to view the room in a detached fashion and then begin the task of taking all the stuff away? How was I to find the strength to move that camera bag, knowing full well that it presently lay where Corey had placed it? It was a horrible thought and even more difficult to execute. Somehow, we found the resolve necessary to begin dismantling Corey's room.

Ally slept in her brother's room from time to time in an effort to maintain contact with him. It became her sanctuary—someplace she could call her own. Months before, we'd formulated an idea for Corey to vacate his room and move downstairs into the spare room so that Ally could move out of the bedroom she shared with her sister. Tom was determined that we follow through on this intention. I had no mind, no energy to dispute his logical decision. However, when it came to putting things away, I was determined that not everything be banished to the closet and hidden, perhaps forever. It was important that I retain and keep in full view some of his more memorable belongings. So what would we do with everything that was our son? Throwing it all in the garbage was out of the question. These things were a part of Corey and always would be. Books were placed into boxes, and the electronic gear he accumulated over the years was packed out to the shed with a vague promise that one day we would sort through it all. Funny—Corey had the same thought. Many times I left his room when the emotions proved more powerful than I could handle.

We decided to place all his personal stuff in the trunk that had once served as a toy box during our family's growing up years. It played the part of a stuffed-animal trunk more than anything else, with a good assortment of broken pencils and stubby crayons; cast-aside coloring books; little cars sporting three wheels instead of four; storybooks without covers; armless, headless, and sometimes legless plastic dolls—toys no longer usable. We cleaned it out and began packing Corey's possessions away. We placed all his clothes in a suitcase. Every article of clothing held very special meaning; he always wore his clothes to the point where we would beg him to toss them out. These were his comfort clothes. Two months before he was killed, we noticed a subtle change in his wardrobe. He began to take pride in how he dressed. We purchased two new sweatshirts for his birthday, and he actually wore them. He had on his bright blue hoodie the day of his accident. The red one, likely not one of his favorites, was worn occasionally. That sweatshirt I commandeered and tucked into my closet.

The Christmas presents he would never use were placed at the bottom of the trunk. This included a new pool cue, his number-one gift request. Next, the set of floodlights we bought for his soon-to-own truck, followed by the soldering iron he would have used to fix all that electronic gear. Finally, we lay his new clothes on top. We sat back and simply stared at the contents of that trunk.

Of course, in the process of going through all the stuff that was in his room, we came across binders filled with old high-school notes and assignments from college as well. These were too personal to put in the recycle box. Written by Corey's hand, they became more priceless than any work created by Picasso. I sorted through his wastepaper basket and retrieved whatever scraps of paper bore his handwriting. I held those sacred pieces of paper to my heart, wishing to imprint them on my soul. As Tom rummaged through Corey's desk drawer, he came upon a sealed envelope, a time capsule written with the firm instruction that it remain sealed until the year 2025. When Tom showed it to me, his immediate reaction was that we respect Corey's wishes. Yet we had very little in the way of personal written communication from Corey. He was a very private person; if he wrote anything down on paper, I knew it came directly from his heart. After some discussion, we decided that it should be opened at once. What was the point of waiting for 2025? The time was now—we needed to hold in our hands something that was a little piece of our son.

With shaking hands and a trembling heart, I tore open the envelope. I read it aloud to Tom. Whether or not Jenn and Ally heard, I cannot say. My voice caught, and the tears stained the page. I had to be careful. This was all we had.

It was dated January 21, 1993 and sealed three days later. Corey began by stating the reason for writing this letter to himself; it was to serve as a memory of his last day of classes for the semester. He reflected on the passage of time, how quickly the years flew by in contrast to the present as he anxiously waited for the bell to announce the arrival of lunchtime. In this same vein of thought, he wrote, "It feels like yesterday I walked into an enormous building, without a clue where to go or what to do. That has passed into the dim dark ages of dust (4 ½ years ago)." The words caught in my throat as I read the most jarring and heart-wrenching sentence I would ever read. "On October 13, 2025, I will be reading what this hand writes, and it seems so far away. No one knows if I will live to be that old." I took a deep breath to stabilize myself, my eyes drinking in the final paragraph. "Little do I realize what a huge world it is out there, and I'm slowly being exposed to this. It will be difficult, but I will make it, and satisfy all of my needs at the same time."

After reading it, I raised my eyes to Tom's and suddenly noticed a newspaper clipping pinned to the wall of Corey's bedroom. It was an article from an advice column, a short piece about self-esteem and rules by which to live. When I read it in the paper a lifetime ago, I wanted to clip it out for myself and save it for future reference. But I got busy and forgot about it. I finally remembered my desire to snip it out, only to find someone had beaten me to it. Now I knew who valued that article as much as I, for there it hung, pinned to his wall.

Corey had dated it on the reverse side, and the words tore afresh at my heart. It read as follows:

1. I refuse to be shackled by yesterday's failures.
2. What I do not know, I will no longer allow to intimidate me. I will instead view it as an opportunity.
3. I will not allow others to define my mood, my method, my image, or my mission.
4. I will pursue a mission greater than myself by making at least one person happy that he or she saw me.
5. I will not tolerate self-pity, gossip or negativism—from myself or from others.

We tucked it in the trunk with the rest of his belongings.

With everything boxed up and stowed away, Ally permanently moved into Corey's room. She chose to keep his room the way he arranged it and even opted for his bed instead of moving and setting up her own. She erected a shrine, which she called her Corey Corner. The mementos included the framed picture and poem she received after Corey's service, a glass rose, and a piece of the grillwork from the front of his car. She told everyone that no one should touch her shrine.

The days endlessly blended together, and I wondered what life was all about. I felt as if I were in limbo, waiting for something to happen. No comfort could be found in memories. There was no word from the police, and the telephone became ever silent. We made futile attempts to keep busy, but when those attempts failed, life let us know it relentlessly carried on, not too bothered by the likes of us. Tom returned to work full-time, trying his best to appear normal. He fooled many people. Did he fool himself?

When my boss contacted me, it wasn't surprising, although still unsettling. I was asked to peg down a date for my return to work. When I thought about it, I found that I couldn't figure out when I wanted to go back or even if I wanted to go back. I knew she needed a definitive answer, but I couldn't help myself. And I certainly couldn't help her.

I did, however, make an attempt to venture out of the safe confines of my home and visit my co-workers. The simple act of dressing took more energy than I thought. First of all, I had to decide what to wear, and then I had to actually change out of my bathrobe. Running shoes would take the place of house slippers.

My unexpected visit caused quite a frenzy. However, not long into my stay, an unexpected tsunami of grief engulfed me, rendering me powerless. My knees buckled, and I melted into a puddle of tears and anguish. I was immediately ushered into a room far from curious stares as if I were an embarrassment. I collapsed in a chair, emotionally spent, and cried. I ranted and raved as I said over and over again, "I don't know where my son is. Moms are always supposed to know where their kids are, and I don't know where he is." In a rather clumsy attempt at consolation, I was told very bluntly, "Corey is dead." Well duh, I knew that! Heaven's sake. I desperately needed to know where he was, that he continued to live, that his spirit was alive and well. I needed to know where he lived after he died. Did he float around the earth? Did he stay near his family? Did he simply go somewhere? Where *was* he? Although I became an instant believer in life after death, I lacked knowledge about the afterlife. Was he okay? I could not help him if he was in trouble. I was powerless to protect him. I could not be with him. I could not advise him. I could not ask for his opinion. I felt so alone in my silent torment as these questions remained sealed within my soul.

This blatant display of raw emotion was more than these women were prepared to handle. So instead of comfort and understanding, I received a few "helpful" suggestions. "Karen, you should consider going on medication. People are worried about you." I prided myself on doing just the opposite. The rationale behind this decision was simple: I knew I would have to deal with these feelings and face the pain, so I opted to do it now. I understood drugs were a delay tactic. Perhaps drugs would make it easier on the people who dared associate with me. But one day, I would have to give up the medication or become a slave to it. I would be lying if I said I never used medication, particularly tranquilizers—there were times when it became a necessary evil. I spent many sleepless nights, my mind racing out of control, the throttle controlling my emotions thrust into overdrive. At those moments, I spun off into the unknown depths of the universe, dragged downward by emotions too strong to resist. When I needed medication, I took it. What I promised to avoid was the day-to-day use of antidepressants. I chose to deal directly with my grief. But the question nagged at me—was I to live for the world or was I to live for me? No doubt, it is easier to look at a happy face than one of sadness. But anguish such as I suffered would show. Grief saturated my soul, making it virtually impossible to conceal. Following closely on the heels of advice about medication came the observation that I wasn't progressing like I should be. Is there some sort of scale with marked gradations on it delineating progress? If so, who designed it? This did nothing but drive the hurt deeper. How could I open myself to other people and expect any sort of compassion?

I cut my storm of sorrow short, realizing that if I were to survive the next moment, I needed to beat a hasty retreat. I dried my eyes, swallowed my hurt, and departed from that building as fast as my feet could carry me, without a backward glance. I arrived home safely, pampering myself with a hot cup of tea and a long soak in the tub. Later that day, I received a call from one of the women at work, a lady also caught up in the awfulness of life after the death of her child. Had she been encouraged to contact me and try to talk me out of this? She told me she knew how I felt. How was that possible? Only one person could possibly know how I felt, and I could not say with any sort of certainty what my own feelings were.

Perhaps my deep and urgent need to talk drove people away. Perhaps they were not willing to listen to the same story, fearing they lacked the proper and necessary resources to advise. They mistakenly thought I looked for direction. I wasn't after counsel. What I longed for was a kind and caring shoulder to cry on, a gentle caress to assure me I was not losing my mind, an open mind with a listening heart, and lips wise enough to refrain from speaking. I believed that those extraordinary traits could be found in families, not in the cold confines of a therapist's office, a stranger sitting across the room, drawing out thoughts and feelings for the sole purpose of exploitation and analysis. I certainly didn't want someone telling me about the little girl who lived within. What I needed was simple: I needed a friend.

Meanwhile, my bond with Corey grew in intensity, despite our separation. He was always there. He was a constant, and I could not fathom that he would no longer be around in the physical sense. So I began to do what continues to this day: it started out as a faith that stated quite clearly that although we could not be together at this moment in time, I would hang on, firm in the knowledge that this division would not last forever. I began to look forward to the next moment, for it could easily lead to contact from him in whatever form he chose. I began learning to live without him, but I only had to do it for one moment at a time. Any longer than that, and my emotions unraveled. How I longed to receive a phone call from him, telling me he was okay. But death was not like that. Death was final. I had to believe he was okay, or I would surely go out of my mind.

After that visit to my workplace, I never subjected myself to another again. This marked the beginning of my determination to no longer fake composure for the benefit of others. This commitment would cost me a great deal. People shifted uncomfortably when around me because I chose to behave in a socially unacceptable manner. I stood up to people who wanted to sweep the existence of my son under the rug. He was a part of me, and he always would be.

The cruelest actions inflicted upon me were empty offers of help. Family and friends alike told me to call if I needed anything. I was anxious to define the word *anything*, but I came up empty, for it lacked shape, form, or substance. I sincerely thought these offers of help were genuine. I thought they were extended with the intention that I might actually use them. I found out quite the contrary. I deeply regretted the few times I managed to summon the courage to call.

One bright and sunny spring morning, we received an unexpected call from a stranger. He identified himself as the business manager of the property where Corey's accident happened. He suggested we clean up the site of the accident. The grass, sprouting and growing, needed attention. The scene had remained untouched since that day in December, a span of close to three months. Tom thanked him for calling and set about making plans to return the area to its former state. We gathered some tools and drove to the accident site. We scoured the ground, gathering all the broken remnants of Corey's car. We found a spring coil from the front end, broken pieces, fragments and slivers of his vehicle. We found scraps of fiberglass in the ditch, washed downstream by the winter rains. I gathered each piece and carefully placed it in a bucket as if an archaeological expedition was underway, and these pieces were artifacts from some long-lost society. We groomed the embankment back to normal, but as a reminder we festooned the tree with yellow ribbon and bouquets of artificial flowers. We eventually added a framed picture as well as a poem one of his aunts would write for him on his twentieth birthday. From that moment on, we assumed responsibility for maintaining the area where Corey died. The scar on the tree caused by the van's bumper remains to this day. The edges have softened, but the wound remains open, creating a visual, symbolic picture of my heart.

After only a short time on this journey of heartache and pain, I had learned countless lessons. Many of these involved the emotion called *grief*, as I dismissed and discarded many of the myths created by society. In the old days, I found my personal experience with grief embarrassingly ignorant. It appeared to me then as a short-lived and brief moment in the span of a lifetime. I never knew grief could be so saturating. I never imagined anything hurting this much. I remember in my former life my reaction when someone died. I cried, and I missed them when I realized I would no longer see them, but then my life went on. This is the way of grief for the rest of the world. I always assumed I would feel sad on occasion; I never dreamed it would become my life. As I struggled with it, as I tried to understand it, I arrived at some profound and radically different conclusions. First, no cure exists for grief, nor is there any getting over it. Grief does not go away—ever. Since I accepted these intuitive insights, I found I no longer lived in fear of grief. I suppose my biggest challenge in life will be accepting other people's viewpoints on grief. I need to learn to accept that I am not able to change other people. I cannot force them to see things as I do.

I had experienced other deaths in my lifetime—grandparents and even a young teenage cousin. I felt sad these people no longer existed. I missed having grandparents to spoil me and take me out for treats and goodies. But I had been taught that as people aged, their chances of dying increased. This left me at odds regarding the death of my cousin. She was sixteen when she was killed in a car accident. I knew her, but only barely. My young heart ached for my aunt, and while it briefly touched on my own mortality, I reasoned it away. How unfair, I realize now. What gave me the right to reason away another person's death? I once believed there existed the possibility of healing and getting over the death of someone so loved. But now I know differently. Before I could practice my newly acquired skills, it would take years of patience. I was too involved in sorting things out for myself, unable to figure out how to help other people trapped in the same set of circumstances.

Very few people would openly welcome the opportunity to get to know grief before absolutely necessary. Death will touch each and every one of us, because with life comes the guaranteed price of death. Perhaps if I had been educated about death and grief, I would not have been so lost and consumed. Unfortunately, no classes were offered in mourning. And if there were, what would attendance be like? How many people would actually enroll and attend?

Grief is a very individual emotion. I tend to wear my heart on my sleeve; my husband loses himself in his work. Tom was more able to pretend, and he fooled many people, including me. I felt very alone most of the time and wondered if I was doing something wrong. Because I refused to be typical and handled my grief my own way, I paid an exorbitant price.

I was not allowed to mourn for my son any longer than necessary as deemed by society—a few weeks or a couple of months at best. If my eyes were red from endless bouts of crying, it was not tolerated. I was not encouraged to speak of him. If I chose to do any of those things, I paid the price of ostracism.

The few people who continued to remain by my side desired less and less to hear about Corey or his journey into adulthood. They did not want to talk about the hole in my life. It was far easier to simply ignore both Corey and his death. After all, what was the point? Nothing changed. Why discuss something as futile as a dead person's future? People feared broaching the subject of death, afraid that doing so would upset me. I think in all truthfulness they were more afraid of upsetting themselves. They refused to allow me to lead, because grief is viewed as a weakness. How could a weak person be expected to lead? Attempting to fit back into society while denying my pain involved some very complicated emotions. This tragedy was not something that could be tucked away. It wasn't that the others did not care; this death just didn't touch them in the same way it touched me. I faced it day after day, night after night. Talking was so beneficial; it released the pressure that built up internally while affording me an opportunity to make sense out of the senseless.

Failure to do this drove the hurt deeper and served no useful purpose. As a result, resentments began to take root and bud.

Failing miserably in my bid to be heard, I turned to the world of books. I could not lay my hands on enough material regarding the topic of life after death. I needed to know about grieving, what to expect as a result of grief, what it meant to lose a child. But attached to this list was one condition. I felt the best advice would come from someone in the same place as me. The expert advice I heard from professionals was factual and exact, but it lacked heart. The critical element missing in expert advice was the personal experience that could only be attained by walking through the fire of losing a child to death. I felt a burning need to know how to do this.

I have since learned that there is no how-to. I've also learned that the painful experience of coping with such anguish is very slow, very unpredictable, and often very paralyzing. I found that my state of mind and ability to survive was determined minute by minute. I never knew what would set me off or when the next wave of grief would wash over me. I was no longer in control of my life, if indeed there ever was such a thing as control. The death of my son drastically changed my point of view. Grief is not short-lived. It is not a straight line from one point to the next. I eventually accepted the fact that I would be mourning for the rest of my life.

Who dared to suggest that people were supposed to get over death? Where did the misconception arise that grief only lasted a year? On the other side of this equation, does the joy of a child only last for a year? Does it not continue to grow and blossom with each passing day? But when a child dies, is that same love expected to die and wither as well?

The experience of joy also changed. In the past, joy had been as uncomplicated as experiencing happiness. Today, joy is complex. The pain of grief invaded the place where unbridled joy once lived. What is that new taste? Bittersweet, perhaps? The important thing for me to remember is this new flavor of life stems from the same source. Love is love. Grief becomes the price that is paid for such love.

Chapter Nine

Phantom Sufferings

Where does a parent find the resiliency to carry on living after her child dies? Some fall back on religion, some turn to religion, some succumb to drugs, alcohol or a combination of both, some give up, some die as well, and some rely on an inner faith guidance system. I did not fall back on my religion nor did I take up a new set of religious beliefs. I vowed to steer clear of drugs and alcohol, and though there were many times when I gave up, I did not die. But I did find inner faith and a belief in life after death. This seed of thought formed the foundation of a new conviction that eventually took root and grew.

The only way Corey could communicate with me was through dreams. The first of many occurred five weeks after his death—and sad to say, I was not the lucky recipient. I tried to figure out why Ally was chosen for the first encounter, only to find out later that her young age was likely the deciding factor. Her innocent mind readily accepted encounters at face value. She believed in Corey and welcomed the opportunity to communicate with him in whatever form it might take.

When she told me she had a dream she wanted to tell me about, she grabbed my attention as I listened spellbound to her story.

"I dreamed I died and went to heaven. I saw Corey talking with friends and relatives. I noticed he was wearing his favorite blue sweatshirt, jeans, and socks or slippers. He came over to me and told me he was okay, but he missed his family terribly. He said he wasn't aware of what happened to him and that it felt as if he had been asleep for a long time. He was aware that his head continued to ache more and more. He saw us standing around his hospital bed and shouted to us, "Hey guys! I'm not down there—I'm up here!" I asked Ally to tell me where *up here* was, and she said, "He was in the corner of the room by the ceiling. He wanted me to tell you that he always provides us with lots of hugs. I asked him about the flashing lights on Carlos's car, and he admitted that he was responsible. He meant no harm, Mom; he was just having some fun. He told me something funny then. He told me to make sure the doors in the house are kept open, as he doesn't like to go through the walls. He also told me his biggest regret was that he never got a chance to say how much he loved us. I asked him how he would communicate with us, and he told me he has incredible powers! Our thoughts come from him. He told me I could use his stuff as long as it does not get ruined. He wondered if you liked his Christmas present as much as he liked all the gifts you got for him. Remember the snow? That was Corey! He told me he heard us as we talked to him in the hospital after his accident. He said he was very confused and knew he could not go back into his body. The morning he died, he was no longer in his body. At the end, he told me he was sad to see me go but promised that he would always be there for me and for us."

I knew Corey had not abandoned us. I always felt he lingered on the perimeter, patiently observing us. Ally's dream spurred me on as I hungrily anticipated the opportunity to connect with my son. I was not disappointed. During my dreams, the connection between us was at its strongest, and time spent together became very precious to both of us.

I asked Corey on a daily basis to show me where he was, and eventually he rewarded me. I dreamed he was with me, although I couldn't see him. I was led to the edge of somewhere that felt like an empty land, a place devoid of human emotion. It seemed very calm, very peaceful, and very desolate. I attempted to step forward, but when I tried, something held me back. Corey whispered that I could not go there, at least not yet.

I found I would be inundated with visits from him while I slept, followed by long stretches of dreamless slumber. I wondered what he did, where he was when not visiting me. I clearly recall our time together, but mostly I remember the vividness of the colors. He always wore the same clothing, although his sweatshirt and jeans were more brilliant. He never spoke, but his thoughts were crystal clear. Before he left, he always asked for a hug and then faded away like a rainbow, slowly vanishing before my eyes.

Ally and I shared a unique bond when talking or communicating with one another. Ours was an easygoing relationship. Jenn and I, however, had to work harder in maintaining our consanguinity. When we connected, it was magical. Between her schoolwork, boyfriend, and extracurricular activities, she rarely had time for anything else. I headed out the door one day for a walk when Jenn asked if she could join me. I decided this might be a good time to delicately broach the subject of her brother. I always wanted to talk about him but felt I needed to tread carefully when bringing up such a delicate topic. She confided to me the difficulty she experienced with this new life; she couldn't make sense of it. As we walked, she said, "When people die, they like to be around those that mean the most to them. They will attempt to talk to you, and if you listen, you can hear them. But because they no longer have a voice, they have to be creative in the way they speak. They do this through songs on the radio, lights flashing, thoughts popping into your head, dreams, and that unexplainable feeling that someone is standing just beyond your field of vision." Little did she know she was presenting me with an incredible gift of validation and reassurance.

The arrival of spring marked the passing of one season and the birth of another. Four months had passed since Corey's death, and April, my birth month, meant one more occasion that would have to be celebrated without him. I reflected back on my birthday of the previous year. I was turning forty, and Tom made quite a show of it. He arranged for a yard card, a proclamation to all that my special day had arrived. There on our front lawn stood these cardboard penguins, forty in total. When I caught sight of my surprise that morning, I kept repeating, "Oh no! Oh no!" Corey couldn't resist—he had to know the cause of such commotion, and he barreled downstairs to see what the fuss was about. When he saw all the penguins, he immediately started laughing. I playfully punched him in the shoulder and said,

"Sure, laugh. Just you wait till you turn forty. Then we'll see who laughs harder." Now I would celebrate my forty-first birthday feeling twice my age. How could I possibly endure a birthday without Corey? Sadly, it became a day like all the others, one that I had to survive.

Two weeks after my birthday, Mother's Day stared me in the face. I couldn't help but think back to my last Mother's Day and the delightful splendor heaped upon me. Tom had taken the kids to the nursery to select a few things. Of course, once Tom started shopping, he had a very hard time stopping. He arrived home with a few things, all right—enough bedding plants to turn the yard from a green landscape into one where every color imaginable graced the flowerbeds. Corey chose a wisteria for me as well as a rhododendron.

A year later, Jenn was working and Tom was called out to attend to an emergency, so Ally and I were left to fend for ourselves. At loose ends and feeling sorry for myself, I turned to Corey, asking for a little help. I wanted to find a way to cope. Before I knew it, Ally and I had engaged ourselves in a game of hide and seek. Tom came home while we were playing, laughter ringing through the house. I couldn't remember enjoying a game so much. We hadn't touched down to earth long when Tom whisked us off to pick up my Mother's Day gift. Tom knew how much I loved flowers, so he arranged a trip to pick up a few hanging baskets. He said his choices were tagged with blue ribbons. Upon our arrival, we were greeted by Dan, who owned the nursery. He excused himself and returned shortly carrying two hanging baskets, one in each hand. Tom decided to help him and left, arriving with two more. As the baskets were laid before me, I watched in wonder as I became completely surrounded by more color than I ever thought possible. When Dan and Tom finally finished their floral march, I counted nineteen baskets in all. But which basket did Corey choose? His passion lay with the wild and exotic; plain and ordinary were not in his vocabulary. He did, however, have a particular fondness for marigolds. As I looked around, I wondered which one was his.

Have you ever heard of a squash basket? Until that day, I hadn't, either. A squash basket contains all the usual plants—heliotrope, anagallis, geranium, giant snowflake, phlox, lobelia, petunia, zinnia, diascia, verbena, scaevola, skylover, ageratum, coleus, and for good measure, impatiens—but when planted, this basket also featured a squash. When Tom had made his selections the evening before, he noticed this particular basket and thought it would make an ideal gift, only to find that someone had already tagged it. As Dan added it to our plethora of plants, Tom stopped him, telling Dan it was not one of ours. Dan asked him, "Weren't all your baskets tagged with blue ribbons?"

Tom replied, "Yes, but that one has an orange ribbon. I checked last night."

Dan said, "No it doesn't," and held it up for Tom. A blue ribbon hung from the bottom. This was, without question, my gift from Corey. And in the fall, the squash revealed its hidden identity. Three tiny, perfect pumpkins adorned its vines, one for each of my children.

That first summer without Corey was riddled with painful memories. All I could do was dwell on the previous summer, how we had camped while Corey stayed behind, content to be left on his own. After he drove Jenn and Carlos out to stay with us for a few days, I ached when it was time for him to leave. But I decided not to push it; we encouraged independence, and at nineteen, he didn't need to hang around with Mom and Dad. So with pain in my heart and a lump in my throat, I watched as he left. I wish now I had insisted he not return home.

This became the first summer Tom and I did not go camping together. Work continued to provide a release for him, and he quite adamantly insisted he would not be taking any time off. I had finally returned to my job in April and now faced three weeks of holidays. I felt anxious and depressed, yet I was determined not to spend my time moping around the house. I did not want to deal with feelings about family and friends any longer. The weather too hot to bear, the house stuffed to overflowing with memories of the previous year, I remained firmly entrenched in the past, a place I felt most comfortable, a time when we were a complete and whole family unit, a time when my son lived. An escape from reality was what I sought.

Instead, I formulated a plan to take Ally on a camping trip. Equally as agitated as I, she leaped like a tree frog at the suggestion when I mentioned my thought to her, encouraging me. Small bursts of positive energy would flood into my heart, saying yes, camping was the right thing to do—but deep bouts of paralyzing fear quickly followed. I began to concoct all sorts of excuses why we could not go. There was too much work involved; the wait was too long to get into the campground; the weather was rainy; I had no energy for such an endeavor. But somehow, some way, we did it. We gathered our resources and went camping for a week. It turned out to be one of the best things I would ever do.

I spent my time away from home reading, playing cards, and sunbathing. Because the campground was so central, nieces came to visit as well as Harriet, my neighbor who worked at the park. I craved my husband's company, but I would have to learn to do without him.

The campground, a leisurely twenty-minute trip from our house, afforded me the convenience of nipping back home for supplies when I ran low. On one of my visits to replenish, Tom was home, and I asked if he would come up and visit with me. He was hesitant to say yes, probably because he felt I abandoned him. It took some persuasive talking on my part, but I finally managed to convince him. He followed behind me in our van, and as we made our way north, I turned to Corey for some divine intervention, some earthly reason why Tom would not be able to return home that night. As I glanced in my rearview mirror, I noticed the van's headlights were not on. I hesitated to mention this to Tom in case something was wrong with them, and he would use this as an excuse to leave early.

We had a wonderful time together, and after dinner, we sat around the campfire enjoying one another's company as the sun slowly bade us goodnight, painting the sky with soft strokes of pink, orange, and purple. Tom rose to his feet, anxious to leave for home. I insisted he stay the night, but he would not hear of it, determined that this would be my time away, not ours. He'd brought me a teddy bear, something to keep me warm at night. He told me I ran away from home, and although he was thankful I had not run far, he insisted that this be my time alone. Maybe he was right, but still, I did not want him to leave. Then I asked him if he had the headlights on during the trip up. He predictably replied, "Yes." I revealed my secret to him, pressing my advantage. If they weren't working, perhaps it would be better if he stayed. He could hardly argue the point, but he did anyway. He diagnosed the problem, fixed the headlights, and left for home.

Ally and I enjoyed the few remaining days left to us. As much as I detested the thought, work beckoned me to return.

Work should have provided a diversion from my grief, but in fact, it was just the opposite. Tensions rose like a tide; people couldn't understand that I was not the same person I once was, and they grew to resent it. In human nature, people craved consistency. Amazing how everyone expected that a death of this magnitude would not change me. I was a fractured person, severed from my child—like an amputation, the limb no longer attached but the pain of the detachment unbearable. It felt like phantom pain. Phantom sufferings. My frustration lay in the way people viewed me. I recall the advice from one lady I worked with. She said perhaps I should throw myself down the stairs. In all likelihood, I would break my leg, and people would have compassion for me, as now I had a physical injury. Everyone would then understand my pain. But if I had no missing limbs, no cuts and scrapes, then I must be fine. What they couldn't see was the raw and ragged hole in my heart, hurting in more ways than could be defined.

One day at work, a casual acquaintance approached me and asked, "How's it going?"

I was so tired of pretense, I asked her what she meant by "it."

"Your life," she said.

Here lay the perfect opportunity to say what I actually thought. I told her the truth. "It continues to be difficult, for it never goes away."

I received the heartless response, "What? Still?"

I could never make her or any other person understand. She turned away from me, shaking her head. As she walked down the corridor, I added, "The best I can ever hope for is to one day learn how to live with this pain." As soon as I spoke the words, I realized how true they were. In spite of everything, I began to learn how to live with a broken heart.

Much like weeding my garden, I continued to separate the good friends from the bad. One of my closest acquaintances lived over five thousand kilometers away. When we lived in Ontario, Denise and I became extremely close despite the fact that we were sisters-in-law. Our relationship extended back to the time before Corey was born. Her daughter Tammy arrived nine days before Corey. When I became a mom for the first time, Denise always helped me over the hurdles. We shared so many things. We spent countless evenings together exchanging stories, gaining knowledge and experience from one another, drinking coffee and basking in the glory of each other's company. Neither of us worked at that time, so we were known to chat late into the evening. Our children grew up together. Those were good times, probably some of the best times of my life.

When we moved to British Columbia, leaving Denise behind was the hardest thing. I remember confiding in her a short time before we left how unsure I felt about our move; was it the right thing to do? She was never one to work a situation to her advantage. In this case, had she told me we were making the biggest mistake of our lives, I would have listened and reconsidered the huge life change we contemplated. Instead, she told me that if I did not go, I would always wonder "what if." I held her words close to my heart and carried them with me to British Columbia.

Denise and I communicated very little after our move, but it did not seem to matter. I knew she would be there when I needed her. In 1985, her husband, Dennis, died suddenly. Without hesitation, Tom and I hopped on a plane and flew back to Ontario. Dennis was one of Tom's older brothers, but Denise was much more than a sister-in-law. She was my best friend.

We flew into Winnipeg in the middle of winter, met at the airport by one of Tom's brothers-in-law, and proceeded to make our way to Kenora. As soon as we arrived, I immediately rushed to her house. I found Denise surrounded by her own immediate family, including their three children. She broke away and scrambled for the safety of my arms. I held her, crying with her, trying to calm and reassure her, letting her know I would remain as long as she needed me.

After Dennis's funeral, all family members arranged to gather at Tom's sister's home. What about Denise? Would she be there? I was told that Denise had her own family around her and that it was best if we left her alone. Who would benefit from this exclusion? I knew where I wanted to be and wasted little time in getting there. I excused myself and hurried to Denise's house. As we sat quietly together, she confided how alone she felt. She wondered why people failed to come back to her house, offering comfort to her and her children. Instead, Dennis's sister removed the focus from Denise and placed it on herself. Would it have been too much to invite Denise over to her home? I wonder why she was never asked.

We remained in Ontario for a week, and every day, if I didn't visit her, I talked to her on the phone. It hurt so much when we returned home.

Denise had a difficult time transitioning from wife to widow, and I wished I could have been there for her. She remarried shortly after Dennis's death, terrified of being alone, widowed at the age of thirty-two with three children to raise—little wonder she was scared. About six months after Dennis died, she called to ask if Tom and I would agree to be guardians for her children in case something happened to her. Dennis's death forced her to face her own mortality. The amount of courage it would have taken her to make that phone call was more than I would ever possess in my lifetime. Her request terrified me. I couldn't face the thought of losing my best friend.

Between 1985 and 1989, Denise and I exchanged the occasional letter. We shared the same birthday, and she always knew my heart was with hers on our special day. I remember writing to her one year and asking her to join me in a birthday wish complete with the happy birthday song at an agreed hour and a toast to each other's good health, happiness, and continued good times. I could picture our voices as they floated across the prairies, mine travelling east and hers moving west, blending together as one somewhere in Saskatchewan.

In 1989, we decided to return to Ontario for Christmas. We told our children about snow and what Christmas was like in Ontario, of warm family gatherings, an incredible feast, and how special that made Christmas. That year marked the end of southern passenger rail service, so we felt very fortunate as riders on the last Via train. What an incredible trip. When we stepped off the train in Winnipeg, bitter cold greeted us. We stood outside the train station waiting for our rental vehicle to show up, huddling together in an effort to generate some body heat. Except for Corey—he stood apart from us and indulged himself in the moment. He said, "This is where I belong." That comment floored me, because he hated the cold. Maybe he felt a special affinity with that part of the country, as it was his birthplace. As we stood on the corner of Portage and Main, blood freezing in our veins, the sight of Corey standing so bravely in the biting cold warmed my heart.

We bunked at my mother-in-law's house for the duration of our stay. We visited for ten days, and the kids cherished every moment of it. Denise was aware of our plans, and I looked forward to her visit. It would have been difficult for her to maintain any ties with her former in-laws now that her connection to them was severed. She told me she no longer felt she was Anne's daughter-in-law, not because she was unloved or unwelcomed, but because Denise lacked the energy required to pretend and carry on while dealing with the painful fact that Dennis was no longer around. As wonderful a family as Tom's was, they preferred to pretend as if nothing tragic touched their lives. When Denise arrived at Anne's house, she and I connected as if we had never been apart.

This would be the last time I would visit with Denise in Ontario. We returned in 1993 for a family reunion and birthday celebration for Tom's mom, but although Denise made plans to attend, somewhere along the way, she changed her mind. I could not blame her, as I probably would have made the same choice. With her second marriage failing, I knew the last thing she looked forward to was facing former in-laws and pretending all was well. I should have called her and made an effort to see her, but I didn't, and I deeply regretted this decision.

In early 1994, Denise received a diagnosis of lung cancer. She wrote a letter to me about all the tests she endured, admitting her terror and fear of the unknown. She was a heavy smoker, but cancer provided her with the incentive she needed to kick the habit. She began to do battle in the fight of her life. She underwent treatment, determined to be victorious, not allowing herself to think the cancer would win. During all this stress, she began divorce proceedings after finding a new and wonderful man. I truly hoped she would attain the happiness she so rightly deserved.

Six months after Corey was killed, Denise came out west for a visit. Years before, she had made the same trip, arriving in Vancouver to visit her daughter. She called then to say she would like to come over to the Island. I waited anxiously for days afterward for the call that never came. This time, when she phoned to say she had made it to Vancouver, I refused to hang up until she promised she would be over to see me the next day. I hardly needed to bother, so strong was her determination. When she and her partner arrived, I answered the knock at the door, wondering who this stranger was who stood before me. The treatments had a devastating effect on her. Not only had her physical appearance changed, but also her voice was different, altered by the radiation. Still, when we embraced after a separation of five years, I knew I held my very dear, my best friend, and nothing would ever change that.

We spent a wonderful afternoon together, and when Denise announced their intention to stay over for the night, my heart sang. The twenty-four hours together were packed with as much living as possible. Tom and I became professional tour guides as we escorted them around our idyllic city. We walked beneath towering cedars on hard-packed trails cuddled next to gurgling streams. We consumed delectable ice cream at a country farm market; we strolled along the waterfront; we drove to the best sightseeing spots to provide them with an unobstructed view of the mainland and distant mountains; we talked, prepared dinner together, and completely indulged ourselves in one another's company. During one of our treks into the wilderness, I noticed Denise quickly tiring. So in tune with her pain and the difficulty she experienced, her boyfriend offered to carry her.

Denise would not hear of it. She never complained, gritting her teeth and leaning a bit more heavily on his arm.

The next morning, Denise's partner excused himself, expressing a desire to take some pictures. He promised to return in time for breakfast. Tom ran an errand, providing Denise and me with the perfect opportunity to speak to one another from the heart. I broached the subject of death and the pain of separation by asking her if she missed Dennis. Over ten years had passed since his death. She said yes, it continued to hurt, even though she had a new man in her life. I looked at her and said, "So this is only a drop in the bucket, the amount of time that has passed for me."

She replied, "It's so different, losing a spouse to losing a child. I cannot imagine what it must be like for you. Six months is a drop in the bucket, five years, ten years are only drops in the bucket. It does not get any easier. Rather, you just get used to not having them in your life."

I found her response refreshingly honest. She didn't try to make me feel better with promises of false hope. She stated what she knew based on her own personal experience, which I appreciated and drew comfort from. She tried to understand my struggle and accepted me for the person I became. Not once did she attempt to fix me or offer suggestions on what I should or should not do. She simply listened.

The hours left together that day were numbered just as they had been from the moment we first met over twenty years before. Time continued to slip away, and I knew it would not be long before they would have to leave for the ferry. I frantically tried to delay the moment of departure for as long as I could. Denise, clearly torn between wanting to stay and longing to leave, seemed grateful when the topic of their imminent exodus was introduced. When he uttered the words, "We should try to make the five o'clock ferry," a cold fist of fear knotted my stomach. Now presented with a deadline, I faced the fact that soon she would leave, probably forever. We sat at the kitchen table, drinking our final cup of tea together. Denise turned to him and said, "Well, we better get our butts in gear."

As I rose from my chair to accompany them to their vehicle, Denise suddenly turned to me and said, "You know, you and I have always had a very special friendship." I nodded in agreement as a lump formed in my throat. I told her I always considered her my best friend. She looked at me and said, "And you have always been mine. It never seems to matter how long we have been apart or how long it has been since the last time we talked, we have always been able to connect again, just like that." For emphasis, she snapped her fingers, visually marking the uniqueness of the bond between us. We clung to each other, as if drowning in the same ocean of anguish. The intensity of her embrace confirmed my suspicions. She was giving me a hug to remember for the rest of my life and what remained of hers. As we lingered in the driveway, Denise finally broke the spell of reluctance gripping us all, the unwillingness to part company. She said, "I hate long good-byes. So we'll just say so long." As they backed their vehicle out of the yard, my heart gave a final, painful tug, realizing I would never see her again.

Tom and I returned to the house, picked up our cups, and sat outside in the late afternoon summer sunshine. Neither of us spoke a word until I tenderly asked Tom, "She's dying, isn't she? She came out here to say good-bye, didn't she?"

He could not lie. "Yes, she is. She came out here to see you before she died." He then went into detail about the severity of her illness. Her cancer had returned with a vengeance, spreading to her vital organs, including an inoperable brain tumor, a tumor in her liver, and the original cancer returning to her lungs. The deadly disease, firmly anchored in her body, eliminated any possibility for further treatment. She knew this and accepted her fate.

During the course of one of her chemotherapy sessions, all fear of death vanished. Tom was told that the person who emerged from the treatment room that day was different from the person who entered. Was she provided with some sort of vision of what lay ahead? When I reflected on our time together, the most profound and remarkable aspect that emerged was Denise's aversion to dwelling on her own mortality. She decided to make the best of the time left to her. She accepted the fact that soon she would die and chose to visit with me one last time. What an incredible honor.

I knew without question that Denise's visit to me was a gift from Corey. He knew how much she meant to me. She would travel whatever distance just to help me in any way possible. This spoke volumes to the type of person she was. Even though I knew that she was dying, the heart part of me prayed that she would somehow survive.

I talked to her on the phone twice afterward—once when she called to say that her daughter gave birth to a baby girl while they visited with us, the second and last time in response to a letter I wrote to her.

A few days after she left our home, I felt compelled to write that letter. I wanted this note waiting in her mailbox when she returned home. It took me forever to pen my thoughts and feelings to her, but I knew I had to do it. After I finished, I tucked it away, suddenly unsure of my actions. I doubted the conviction of my words. I asked Jenn to read it over. If she told me it was inappropriate, I vowed I would destroy it. She returned the letter to me, encouraging me to mail it. Before any further apprehensions settled in, I sealed the envelope and deposited it in the mailbox.

Denise's strength waned, but she called me late in August to say she had received my letter. She sounded breathless, as if just completing a ten-kilometer run. She told me she experienced fewer lucid days and had just emerged from a very bad spell. She told me her boyfriend continued to take good care of her, and he was the one who encouraged her to call. He left to run an errand at the store, so she seized the moment to phone. We joked about the admirable job he performed for her and how soon his head would no longer fit through the doorway. Her laugh warmed me like a fuzzy blanket on a cold winter's day. Although she never directly answered the question I posed in my letter, I knew she was calling to say yes.

In my letter, I asked that if she got to heaven before me (and I emphasized the fact that I had absolutely *no reason* to believe that she would), if she would do me the honor of looking after my son until I got there. As one mother to another, I knew I could entrust her with his care, just as she had once asked of me following the death of her husband Dennis. We did not talk for very long as her strength rapidly diminished, and she needed to rest. With a final "I love you. See you later," we disconnected for the last time. Denise died on September 10, 1995.

As summer began its final dance in preparation for the arrival of fall, fierce pain gripped my heart. Corey would have been twenty. We always made a big production of the kids' birthdays. We provided them with a choice of their favorite home-cooked meal or dinner out at their favorite restaurant. They always, without fail, chose the home-cooked meal. Corey's number-one choice was always the same—lasagna, hold the mushrooms.

His birthday arrived, and everywhere were gentle indications that he was near. As the day began to dawn, Tom noticed a rabbit on the lawn, bathed in the light from the kitchen window. Rabbits held special meaning to us. The morning Corey died, I stood at the hospital window in the Intensive Care Unit, watching people as they arrived for work, eyes cast downward, focused on getting to work on time. At that moment, I noticed rabbits emerging from the shadows, softly munching at the moisture-laden grass. Corey loved rabbits. As I wrestled my musing back to the present, I thought, "Here is a rabbit, bathed in the soft glow of early morning, looking into the house at us. How beautiful."

How would we celebrate the birthday of someone no longer around? How could I ignore it? Would I do as suggested—drug myself and hope it passed as quickly as it arrived? We knew Corey, and we knew what he would want. I prepared the yummiest lasagna dinner I could manage; I baked a birthday cake in his honor, crying the whole time. We made birthday cards expressing our anguish on paper. We let him know he continued to hold a valued position in our family. We received cards on his behalf from extended family members who had kindly inquired of our plans ahead of time. Jenn, however, expressed one concern. "You aren't going to buy him presents or anything weird like that, are you?" I assured her that this was not in our plans, as Corey had no use for material objects.

To honor Corey, we drove to the nursery and purchased two plants for him. He possessed a natural ability to grow anything from seed, first demonstrated when he was only two and a half years old. May 1978 had been a cold spring day in Ontario. Corey was playing alone outside and decided he wanted to fish. His dad fixed him up with a makeshift pole to which he fastened a red plastic fish. Tom filled a garbage can and let Corey dangle his pole in the water. Corey's little face lit up with pride when he showed us his catch. He tired quickly of the game, venturing over to his sandbox. I watched as, instead of playing with his cars, trucks, and tractors, he wandered around the yard, gathering twigs from the ground. He returned to his play area, stabbing three small bare sticks into the sand. After he finished, he came to the door calling my name. I asked him what all the excitement was about. He pointed, and I said, "Oh, I see. You have put some branches in your sandbox." Silly person that I was, I failed to see what he had really done.

"No Mommy," he said. "I planted trees." Indeed he had.

Christmas approached, and the inevitable collection of seasonal greeting cards began appearing. Perhaps out of respect for our feelings, Corey's name was omitted. Being on the receiving end of those cards, it hurt to see no mention made of him. Had they forgotten him already? I seized this as sign—relatives needed a little educating. From the time Corey was killed, Tom and I had agreed to include Corey's name with ours. A fluffy cloud encircling his name would be drawn, symbolizing that although he existed on a different plane, he continued to be a cherished member of our family. So I made up little cards with a message explaining our preference for having Corey's name included, offering assurance that it was not awkward or the wrong thing to do. These notes were tucked in with the cards I sent out that year, and as a demonstration, I included Corey's name when I signed the cards. I don't think my wish was very well received. Our desires were ignored and remain so to this day. Perhaps they preferred to forget he ever lived.

Christmas had lost its flavor for me. It became a season of incredible pain and horrible reminders of what had happened. In order to survive, I found I needed to don a thick layer of armor, designed to deflect the hurt raining down on me. This was not easy. I became resentful and angry—I should be Christmas shopping, baking, and decorating the house. But all the magic had been lost.

There was no delight in purchasing gifts, no pleasure in venturing to the mall and looking at all the things that once brought happiness and joy. The lights, the sounds of Christmas and the songs became painful reminders of a season gone horribly wrong. I could not understand the happiness of people. I could not understand how I was to carry on. I could not understand God. Our first Christmas without Corey passed in a blur riddled with excruciating pain. Our second Christmas terrified me. The agony of separation became amplified many times over. In an effort to cope, we arranged to take a trip far away.

Before we left on our excursion, and without warning, Jenn dreamed of Corey. The particular morning it happened, Jenn burst from her room in an explosion of haste, calling my name and plunging headlong down the stairs. As I gathered her in my arms, between heart-wrenching sobs, she told me her dream. She said she was on a bus with Corey when suddenly a lion attacked him. Immediately he was rushed to hospital, and the doctors assured her he would be fine. She was ecstatic—at long last, she had found him. Her only thought was presenting her family with the ultimate gift for Christmas. Our trip to Maui had been finalized, but she knew that purchasing another plane ticket would not present a problem; her dad could do anything. Corey appeared in the doorway to the house as she called me to join with her to witness firsthand this miracle presented before us. She said we were so happy we could not wait for her dad to share in the excitement. The unexpected surprise jolted her awake before her dad could appear. Instantly realizing this was nothing more than a dream, she fled down the stairs, sobbing uncontrollably in my arms. The sound of my daughter's heart breaking was one of the most horrible things I ever heard.

The day of dread finally arrived. One year had passed since Corey was involved in the killer accident. I spent the whole day reliving the past, thinking that nothing had changed in the time since his death. I reprimanded myself for many things—I should have spent time with him, talking to him instead of acting so selfish and self-centered. I wished he had gone to work that day, safely out of harm's way, away from the crushing carelessness of a faceless driver. If he had gone to work, he would be here today.

Christmas morning arrived silently and without fanfare. No anticipation, no early-morning rising, no mad rush downstairs to witness the magic of Santa's passage as he breezed through our house. All was quiet as the girls slept. Gone were the days when they would burst into our room at 5:30 a.m., exploding with excitement and expectancy. Gone were the days when we would tell them they could take down their stockings, but the opening of the presents would wait until a more decent hour. That day, we ate turkey like all normal families, but I have no recollection of stuffing the bird or preparing our dinner. Thankfully, we would be leaving for Maui in three days' time.

Preparing for a trip offered a welcomed diversion for me—the thought of travelling buoyed my spirits, but little did I know, sorrow packed a bag and joined me on our getaway. For the first week and a half, a cloud of gloom and sadness surrounded me. I had placed too many expectations on this trip restoring my battered soul. But if the truth were told, I was enraged because Corey was not there with us sharing in all the tropical splendor. We spent our days on the beach like all the other tourists, but my spirit physically ached. It hurt to see people having fun, sharing good times, and making memories together.

One day, after a rainstorm, we decided to partake in a driving exploration of the island. We chose the west circle route, as it was known for its peace and tranquility. We stumbled upon acres and acres of pineapple fields in pure isolation, far removed from the industrial heart of the island. The resorts thinned out as the road became less congested, taking on a rural feel.

The best part of the whole drive was when we came across a bluff overlooking the Pacific Ocean. On this barren and windblown precipice, people practiced the art of balancing rocks. Mounds of small boulders precariously stacked one upon another in the desolation of the landscape inspired us to do as countless others had done before us. We began to pile rocks, thrilling in the challenge of competing to see whose work of art would tumble and whose would remain standing. Photographs were snapped as we reveled in the observation of our kids acting like the children they were. They cast aside their heavy cloaks of adulthood as giggles and sounds of glee filled the quiet tropical air. No worries and no thoughts of the next moment. There was only now. I smiled.

The wind blew off the ocean, and as I glanced out to sea, I contemplated the vastness of life. As human beings, individually we are specks on the earth. Suddenly, my eyes picked up a tiny movement on the water far below me. I noticed a tugboat as it fought the waves, battling toward an unseen destination. As I focused on it with my binoculars, how dwarfed he became surrounded by the sheer volume of empty water. How could he possibly see where he was going as the ocean rose in towering swells above him? I quickly connected the symbolism to my own life. I was lost in the ocean of life. Where lay my destination? Here I stood, fighting against the same massive waves, battling to stay afloat while fixing my vision on something that would lead me back to life. I needed a reason to want to carry on. I needed to know why I should keep struggling. Sometimes it felt better to allow the waves to wash over me; often I wished they would swallow me just so I would not have to fight any longer.

The pictures I snapped of my family as they built their masterpieces of rocks and pebbles captured looks of concentration and determination. Our task completed, we carefully picked our way back to the car, the rockwork left for someone else to ponder over and admire. As I glanced back across the land one last time, I found I could no longer discern the creations that belonged to our hands. They blended with all the other unsigned works of art. This felt like sacred territory as we stepped over the hard efforts of others, gratified in knowing that we left a little piece of ourselves on that island in the middle of nowhere.

We returned home after two weeks away only to find that things had not changed. Did anyone miss us while we were gone? The only one who welcomed us home was Jenn's cat, Cleo. In the space of one year, I had lost the ability to relate to other people. I kept my sorrow to myself and took great comfort that I could remain true to myself. But I forgot about the rest of my family. The one bad thing about turning inward was that I became used to shedding my tears in private. Tears meant that I hurt, and I did not want my children to witness my pain. I was supposed to be the grown-up and as such remain strong.

Chapter Ten

When Grief Strikes

Grief can strike at any moment, in any place, at any time. Grief is quite capable of taking on the form of something innocent and harmless. Grief came to visit one day disguised as a simple piece of paper folded in half. Not knowing what it was, I opened it and gazed at it, unable to comprehend the significance of what I held in my hand. Immediately upon recognition, I was pitched headfirst into a pit of indescribable despair. What I held was a receipt for a bank deposit Corey made prior to his death. This little slip of paper instantly became sacred to me. That fold, that crease was made by him. His fingerprints were on it. These moments of unprepared discovery would truly become the difficult times, and I wondered how these times could be expected to become easier. Maybe when the chance of stumbling upon mementos left behind no longer appeared, maybe then these unexpected tumbles into grief would cease. I knew when that moment arrived, Corey's death would become very real.

Before I fell asleep that night, the haunting phone call I received from the hospital invaded my semiconscious mind. I could not understand how someone could receive such horrific injuries in so short a span of time. How did he go from healthy and whole to barely functioning in the space of a few seconds? Who held the answer to this question? Who would answer it for me? I felt extremely frustrated as I tried to grasp and comprehend the whole concept. If only someone would answer me. If there were answers, would I be able to understand and make sense of them? Would I want to?

How did he manage to die? What did he do wrong? Was death a punishment? Why?

Crying accomplished nothing, I was told. I wondered what that meant. Tears were a natural response to grief. True, it changed nothing in the world, but emotionally it provided a release for all the pent-up feelings of frustration, helplessness, and anger. I tried to hold back the tears for long periods of time, but ultimately the crying always won. Why was I left to struggle, to carry on in life? That was the cruelest unanswerable question of all.

How could I have imagined that there would be so many opposing emotions inside the single entity that encompassed grief? It left me totally exhausted and emotionally spent when I tried to analyze it. Why did I do this? Why was I the only one who did it? *Was* I the only one who did it? I did not see the rest of the world trying to understand why I became the way I was. It was up to me to try to understand the world.

Life operated on a different schedule—harried and impatient. I operated as if the day had no beginning and no end. We received notice one day that our allowable time limit of two years to settle with the insurance company was almost upon us. That seemed unfathomable, for I could barely grasp the meaning of a single day. Without realizing it, the deadline had been stalking us, patiently waiting for its chance to pounce. Attempts too numerous to count were made to sit down and tally up our lives on paper, painfully placing a dollar figure beside each item and presenting it in a reasonably clear format for the insurance company. How does a parent measure in dollars the value of the life of a child?

When Tom booked the appointment with the insurance adjuster, I thought long and hard about attending. He had taken care of most of the unpleasant details when Corey was killed, and I had not provided him with the love and support he needed and deserved. No question remained in my mind that he would be able to handle this on his own, but why should he? This involved our son, his and mine. I would need to arrange for time off work, possibly incurring wrath along the way, but I would not let this deter me. When I called Tom and told him I would be accompanying him, he sounded relieved.

Unaware that a third party had been listening to what I thought was a private conversation, I jumped when I heard a co-worker say, "Are things going okay with Corey?" Shock and horror filled me. I wondered what that meant. How could anything to do with a child dying be termed as okay? What on earth was she saying? Fortunately for her, I chose to ignore her question. This was neither the time nor the place for any sort of discussion regarding my son.

The vehicle was registered in Tom's name and until we settled with the insurance company, the car was ours to do with as we pleased. Our wish was that it remain undisturbed until we felt better able to deal with all the necessary paperwork and accompanying emotions. That time arrived last September, nine months after the accident, when we assembled as a family and paid a final visit to Corey's car. It sat alone, abandoned in the salvage yard awaiting its final fate. Time and the elements had imposed their will on the tangled, rusting heap of metal. The girls gasped audibly when they witnessed firsthand the damage inflicted on his small blue vehicle. It barely looked like a car. As we approached it reverently, I watched as Corey's sisters began to circle it, disbelief registering on their sweet young faces. We searched through it one last time to retrieve any personal items. We found the calculator we gave him on his nineteenth birthday, his first-aid kit (how ironic that discovery seemed), the grey blanket that was burned (how did it come to be that way?), a copy of his resume (there was his name, in black and white!), the license plate, some other personal papers, and his most prized possession—his stereo. Although the stereo was smashed and no longer usable, Jenn said she wanted to keep it, if only because Corey had bought it. It proved to be difficult to extract from the wreckage, compressed into the dashboard by the force of the collision. I removed the gearshift knob, which had meant so much to Corey. He wanted it then, and I wanted it now. We peeled off the pin striping from both sides of the car for reasons unknown. We peeled off the Toyota windshield sticker for the same unknown reason. This was all we had left of him, and when this car was towed away, another part of him would be erased forever. Then, as now, reality refused to sink in even as it stared me in the face. As we turned to leave with heavy hearts and tear-stained cheeks, we murmured,

"So long little blue car." In all the time that passed, nothing changed. His car was still destroyed, and Corey was still dead.

Now here we were once again, tidying up the financial loose ends. It was the only thing that the world seemed to understand. Money made everything okay. Never mind the emotional heartache and the devastating emptiness we carried with us every single day. Money talked. We eventually received compensation for lost wages and general expenses. All related travel and engineering costs were ours to bear. Also included was the car loan we had taken out on Corey's behalf. Tom co-signed for Corey and insured the loan but in the wrong name. Neither was the accrued interest on the loan eligible for reimbursement. We were told we should have settled this earlier. So what if we were unable to pull our financial thoughts together long enough to actually deal with the loan and pay it off. Who cared? Not the bank, not the insurance company. They only dealt with figures on paper. Did they care about the heartache and misery we experienced every time we looked at funeral bills and ambulance bills? Did they care about the grief that arrived in waves, relentlessly pounding on our emotions? Did they care about the tearstains on the paper obliterating everything we had written down? Did they care about the countless hours spent writing how important Corey was to us and his role in our family? Did they care that it actually required more time for us than they thought it *should* for such a simple undertaking? We should have been able to do it sooner. We should have been able to put our hearts aside long enough to complete this uncomplicated assignment. What was wrong with us? Were we to say, "To hell with emotion, to hell with feelings—just get the job done?" Apparently so. We were punished for our inability to deal with these cold hard facts. The driver who caused all this carnage in our lives—where was he? Well, he wasn't in Nanaimo. Following the collision, he closed his business and fled to another province. In fact, the state attorney asked the court to issue a cross-Canada warrant for his arrest to face charges resulting from the crash. So he ran away and hid like a coward while we remained behind struggling to put back the pieces of a life we no longer recognized. We were the ones left to face reality.

Chapter Eleven

Searching for Answers

As if suffering the death of my child wasn't enough, I was forced to endure a whole host of additional trials ranging from the expected to the brutal. I found that the only people who really wanted to talk to me were those who were ignorant of my tragedy. The instant they knew, they immediately withdrew, as if they could actually catch death from me. Often, a simple answer to an innocent question triggered their retreat. "So, do you have any children? Where are they now?" I have never been one to tell a lie, and I knew I could not start now. So I told the truth and suffered the consequences. Should I have kept my secret hidden? I didn't know how I was supposed to do that. I did not know how to handle society, and society in turn did not know what to do with me.

I became an outcast because my child died. Where did I fit in? I used to have my own niche; not only had someone moved it, but also it had changed into something unrecognizable. I felt too old, too tired to begin searching for a new one. The world seemed full of carefree people, and how I envied them. I found that I stepped cautiously, as if my life's path were littered with land mines. Grief followed me relentlessly day after day. It pursued me in my dreams. There was no escape.

Our home life felt like it was falling apart. Instead of one complete unit, we were now four individual people trying to cope as best we could in a heartless world. We used to think alike, do things together, and enjoy our time together; at the same time, we were comfortable when apart. We were now splintered, and nothing could make us whole again. Corey was the bond that had held us together. He provided so much to each of us that we weren't aware of until he was gone. Now the four of us existed together, but it was as if we had forgotten how to be a family.

I never thought I would miss the joy of grocery shopping. Only when I had to resume this monumental task did I realize the amount of energy it demanded. It was not simply the act of walking up and down aisles that consumed me. It was the incredible brainwork involved in putting together a simple grocery list. I had to methodically plod through the cupboards and pantry with pen in hand as I tried to envision what grocery items I needed to buy. Food and cooking had lost their appeal, and shopping became drudgery.

Another year crept by, and before we knew it we were looking at Corey's birthday once again. The person disappeared, yet the day of his birth hadn't. Early that morning, I awakened and crept out of bed, careful not to disturb Tom. Once downstairs in the living room, I gazed at the gradually brightening sky. Dawn was breaking, the birds were beginning to sing, and the final traces of nightfall were reluctantly retreating. This was how Corey's birthday should be. It reflected perfectly his personality—soft and unimposing. It felt so empty that he was not here with us, embracing the day. Tom rose shortly afterward, and we snuggled together on the sofa. We spoke of many things, of life, death, people, and work. Then we regressed and remembered another very painful time. We spoke about Tom's work-related accident that happened in 1983.

On a Tuesday following a long weekend in August, Tom returned to work after a two-week camping vacation with our children. I remember receiving the phone call that fateful day. I remember the sense of calm I felt. I handled myself in a very rational manner, largely because the information I was given lacked detail. I was told Tom had sustained a fall from a ladder but would be okay. I found this puzzling, because his mind was always on his job, and it had to be when working with electricity. I was told to make my way to the hospital. What I did with our three children remains a blank. I arrived at the hospital well in advance of the ambulance that transported my husband.

The exact extent of his injuries remained unknown to me; in fact, as I sat alone in the reception room anxiously waiting for his arrival, all I could think about was how embarrassed he must have felt falling off his ladder. I felt sure he had suffered only minor injuries, with perhaps his dignity sustaining the most bruising. Only when I saw his boss's face did it register—this was not a case of merely slipping from a ladder.

Tom had been standing at the top of an aluminum ladder that straddled a metal-and-glass jewelry display case. The floor beneath him was concrete and tile. Before ascending the ladder to deal with the wiring behind the suspended ceiling twenty feet above him, he had manually disabled the disconnect switch at the panel. For some unknown and unexplained reason, the store's computer overrode the safety switch and turned the power back on. As he reached for the wires to reconnect them, the electricity entered his body, searching for a path to the ground. Helplessly welded in its powerful grip, Tom was held fast while wicked current poured into his body. Luckily, he had enough presence of mind to realize that touching the aluminum ladder with his free hand meant certain death. The only option left for escape involved pushing himself off the ladder.

While all of these thoughts raced through his mind, he begged someone to help him, but the saleslady could not understand why he needed help. No one could see the invisible energy as it burned its way through his hand, arcing between his fingers. The saleslady watched in abject horror as he fell twenty feet, landing on the display case before crashing to the floor. Fortunately, he did not land on his back. His left hip absorbed the impact of the fall, and his femur suffered a fracture below the hip socket.

Upon his arrival at the hospital, I anxiously approached him as the emergency-room staff proceeded to assess him. He lifted his head from the stretcher while holding an oxygen mask firmly to his face. He feebly but bravely raised his injured hand in a sad attempt to wave to me so I would know he was okay.

After our family doctor conducted a preliminary examination, he walked briskly to where I stood in the waiting room. As soon as I heard the word "arced," I froze instantly, realizing that my husband had suffered electrocution.

A very long recovery period lay ahead of Tom. He would be off work for six months. He lay in the hospital for six weeks before being discharged home. Vigorous physiotherapy filled his day. I had been accepted into a college program, and though I didn't want to, we were forced to carry on with this plan as money had already been committed.

As with all stressful situations, it took a while before I allowed myself the time I needed to explore the reality of what had happened and what could have happened. With the kids safely tucked in bed for the night, I slipped out to the back patio. This felt like a safe haven to shed some tears and release some of the pent-up emotions boiling inside. At that particular moment, my neighbor came over and caught me red-handed. She felt the driving need to pass along unsolicited advice. She told me, "You have to buck up and pull yourself together. Crying does no good and serves no purpose. It will not change your situation one bit." I dried my eyes and resolved that I would never let anyone catch me crying again. Tears were regarded as shameful and a display of weakness.

Meanwhile, Tom waged his own personal war. He was so severely affected in a psychological sense that he found his view of life permanently altered. He recovered physically, but something continued to nag at his conscience. He became a man possessed, and the reason for this change would not be revealed for years. Instead of resting and allowing nature to heal his broken leg, he chose to spend every moment he could with his family. He had always been a devoted father, but suddenly time became a precious, valuable commodity. He doted on his children and played with them during his recuperation in spite of the crutches he used. We ventured to the park for strolls during the early fall. Inevitably, we ended up pelting one other with soggy orange and yellow leaves. The six months he spent at home recovering were lived to the fullest. I remained true to my pledge of returning to school with the hope of securing a job after graduation. We maintained our household, and I eventually managed to find an ideal part-time job.

But Tom was a changed man. This transformation to his personality meant that he was often angry and depressed. The doctor felt he suffered post-traumatic stress as a result of his accident, but Tom knew this was not the case.

I struggled as I pulled my thoughts back to the present. Tom chose that moment to reveal the secret he had been keeping for over thirteen years. Somehow, he was granted a glimpse of the future as he lay helpless in his hospital bed, a future that did not include Corey. Now I understood the reason behind the driving need to be with his family and watch over his son as much as he could. This explained fully his anger and protective spirit as he fought to change what he felt was certain to happen. As I listened, I wished he could have found a way to keep Corey safe.

Sadness engulfed me as I remembered once again that it was Corey's birthday. I suddenly developed a burning need to buy twenty-one yellow roses, one for each of Corey's years. The first florist I called had twelve, but I needed nine more. As I leafed through the yellow pages, my eye caught an ad that sounded familiar, but I couldn't say why it captured my attention. The lady who answered the phone said she would check her stock and returned to tell me she had only nine roses—the exact number I needed. Could this be a coincidence? I didn't believe in coincidence. That word was used a bit too freely to explain away instances in life that seemed guided from beyond.

After we picked up the flowers from the shops, we made a trip to the accident site. The ribbons hung in tatters, crying for replacement. We cut down everything, strung fresh ribbon, and laid down the glorious sunshine-yellow flowers at the base of the tree. While we were attending to this, Tom set up the video camera to record our moment in time. The car radio had been left on, and only when we watched the movie later did we hear the words, "I will remember you."

That evening, we ate the lasagna I knew he would have wanted as his birthday meal. We set a place for him at the table and lit a candle for him. I gazed at it as we ate dinner in silence. It flickered. I wondered if this meant he was near. Choking back tears, we sang "Happy Birthday" and cut his cake. As I placed the last forkful of food in my mouth, the flame on the candle suddenly went out. It took a few moments for me to decipher the message that came through. It would be just like my son. "Got to go, Mom. My friends are waiting." And he would be gone.

After dinner, we prepared to make one final trip back out to the tree to retrieve the flowers. The temperature outside had dropped, and the wind began to blow as we made our way out into the cold, unforgiving night. As we approached the scene and stopped the car, I was consumed with disbelief as my eyes fastened on the sight before me. A complete rainbow of chrysanthemums in every color created embraced the tree and spread across the lawn. We gathered the roses to take home but left the mums to shine softly in the night.

With the arrival of December came the inevitable family gathering at Tom's sister's house. We were expected to attend. We were asked to forget our heartache and put in an appearance for the sake of other people. I felt empty and hollow inside. To attend would have required untold amounts of pretense followed by generous portions of deception. I found these two ingredients sorely lacking in my desolate heart. I knew that surely condemnation would follow. "For goodness sakes, it's been two years already. Surely they are over this by now and have returned to normal." And closely on the heels of that thought stalked rebellion. I knew there would be no return to *normal*. Neither would there be any *getting over* this.

Relatives had very little use for us during the rest of the year. The phone had ceased to ring long ago, and they assumed we were fine. At a time of year when we could have used a little compassion and understanding, not a shred was to be found. We were in a season of mourning. This was the time of year when the pain became so large, so magnified, and so intense that no amount of medication could dull it. It hurt to see complete and whole families, knowing that Corey would not be showing up.

Being alone became a way of life for me. It's not that I expected other people to be in mourning. After all, their child had not been killed. Perhaps if I had received some acknowledgement of Corey's absence, it would make pretending a little less painful. But instead, he was ignored, and so was my family's pain.

If only *the others* could have taken my cue as I tried to honor their Christmas traditions. If only they could have respected and honored my decision to abstain from the family gathering that year. Everywhere I went, memories of Corey met me at every turn. Everywhere I turned, I expected to see him. Every time I turned around hoping to see him, I gazed instead upon empty space, and my heart plummeted to earth once again. It went on and on, this revisiting of my grief.

People needed so much to believe that we were okay. They would feel so much more comfortable if they could keep their distance from the hurt so raw and the grief so real. Separation was their protection, but it was my prison. How could we connect? Or would the chasm of death alienate me from everyone forever?

Chapter Twelve

The Solace of Tears

Christmas gnawed at my heart while time reminded me that we had to sit down and write our Victim Impact Statements, our only voice in the upcoming trial involving Corey's accident.

With pen firmly poised, the law began to write the final chapter in the story of this horrific accident. Blame would be assigned, and punishment would be meted out. But in the latest turn of some very ugly events, we suffered another injustice. We had waited almost two years for some form of restitution, when ideally we sought retribution. During that time, the accused chose to toy with us. After being served with a warrant, he entered in a plea of "not guilty." A few weeks before the case was scheduled to proceed, a guilty plea to the lesser charge of failing to stay right of center was entered. There was no mention in this menial charge of the death this coward caused, and neither was there any provision for an attachment. I felt as if we had been sold out. The prosecution was quite anxious to accept this guilty plea. A condition was attached to the plea bargain—the second charge of driving without due care and attention would be dropped. I listened incredulously as this information was relayed to us. To have my child killed was one thing; to have to endure his death without acknowledgment was another. The upcoming court appearance was merely a formality. The guilty plea would be officially registered, and a date for sentencing would be set. We stood firm in our decision to face this together, to present a united front. This was the pledge we made at the very beginning: we would stand as one.

The Victim Impact Statement was the only crumb in the whole loaf of the justice system allowing us to express the effect of Corey's death. I could not imagine the time and effort it must have taken to initiate and move the system in the direction of acknowledging the victim's pain. Thankfully, someone did. If not for Victim Impact Statements, the cries of the walking wounded and shell-shocked would have continued to be silent.

Where would I begin? How could I articulate what my son meant to me? How could I convey the depth of the sadness I felt? How could I accurately bring to life the terror in my soul as I anxiously waited at the hospital for a miracle that never came? How could I express my feelings effectively, providing a glimpse of the devastation in my life? How could I accurately project on paper the sense of incompleteness we now suffered? The pain of each new day needed to be stated to precisely reflect the anguish in knowing Corey would no longer be around to share anything with us ever again. I needed to make it clear that no matter how many times we were told at the hospital that no hope remained, we never gave up on him. The horror of the words *brain dead* needed to be brought to life. Where would I begin to put down all these thoughts while keeping emotion at bay?

We were supplied with ready-made forms that consisted of a few lines to fill in and present back to Victim Services. We cast aside the forms and wrote from our hearts. It was a long, laborious, and demanding exercise, but one I felt I owed to Corey. The justice system needed to hear of my pain. We only had a month before the hearing for sentencing was scheduled to take place. One month to try to say what needed to be said in the most effective manner possible. It was both a long time and a short time.

We did not accomplish much at the first sitting. The slow, painful evolution began as disjointed sentence fragments scrawled on paper that over time, eventually, culminated in a multi-page testimony of love. When we compared our final product to the form we had been given, it was quite obvious that one piece of paper would not have been enough.

The law definitely favored the perpetrator. The careless driver was protected and awarded all the rights. We, Corey's parents, had no rights. We had to justify our pain. The accused never needed to utter a word. He could silently stand by and pretend it never happened. He knew he had the law on his side. He knew silence was his best friend, because to admit to anything meant accepting responsibility for his actions. He was not required to say he was sorry. He continued to drive. It was up to us to come to a conclusion for his senseless and careless act. But why should we? Why should we be the ones left to put the puzzle together, to speculate on the reasons behind his actions? How could the law protect the person who committed this act, an act that constituted an abstract form of murder? We were left standing in the pouring rain, placing flowers at the site where Corey had been struck down. Did these thoughts ever invade the mind of the accused?

The second anniversary of Corey's death dawned, and it was difficult to concentrate on anything except what the day signified. We flew to Florida in a bid to escape the pain. While there, we occupied ourselves with sightseeing, but we did not see things through the eyes of tourists. We saw them through eyes misted over with tears. All we had to do was climb over the hump of December, and we would be okay for a few more months. Our spirits would feel a bit more light and our hearts a little less heavy.

While in Florida, we were graced with an amazing spectacle—the last full moon on Christmas Eve until the year 2102. It was rumored that strange and magical things occurred when the moon was full on Christmas Eve. We decided to see if this tale had any truth to it.

No clouds in the sky marred the moon as it shone bright as the star lighting the way to Bethlehem. It looked magical, but it lacked magic. My only wish was to have Corey come back. He didn't.

We spent our days exploring the nooks and crannies and flatlands of Florida. We made a point of searching out an old fort Tom and I had discovered twenty-four years before. All we found were markers where buildings once stood. Time had erased this memory, too.

After ringing in the New Year, I realized we only had one week left of our vacation. Going home was the last thing I felt like doing. There had been no arguments, no fights, and no bitter words between us. We were knitting ourselves together, but returning home meant the stitching would begin to unravel. Our souls would once again be subjected to all the pain we had left behind.

Chapter Thirteen

Our Day in Court

The moment I had been waiting for was quickly approaching. Soon I would set eyes on the person who destroyed our lives. I wondered if he had any distinguishing features, markings perhaps, that would separate him from ordinary people. Did he wear his guilt like a second skin? What sort of person killed another human being and never acknowledged or accepted responsibility for it? Was he capable of feeling guilt? Did his conscience haunt him, or was he able to brush it aside without another thought? How could he not beg for forgiveness?

I applied the finishing touches to my Victim Impact Statement the evening before our day in court and read over the statements written by my husband and children. Ally wrote from her heart—she expressed her feelings without difficulty. Jennifer amazed me the most. She managed to keep her pain carefully tucked from sight; it was hidden so well that I feared for her. She constantly struggled to cope and adjust to a life that no longer included her brother.

This opportunity to express myself opened the floodgates of emotion. I could not write enough; however, the words seemed horribly inadequate. My voice on paper rang hollow in spite of feelings that ran deep. When it came to articulating my thoughts, hopes, dreams, wishes, and love for Corey, the English language lacked eloquence. When I finished, my work felt incomplete, as if the surface of my emotions had barely been scratched.

I was not able to fully appreciate the depth of my husband's pain and anguish until I read his statement. "From this moment forward, every breath would be heavy, every heartbeat a burden." Maybe Tom and I weren't as far apart in our torment as I thought. Maybe I happened to be a little more vocal in expressing myself, and he was a bit more silent.

Why did I feel like I was the one about to receive a sentence? I glanced at the clock and realized that in twelve hours, we would know. This part of our lives would pass, and we would know the punishment one received for killing an innocent person. True, every case is different, but there should be a standard provision in the law dealing with careless driving that causes death.

The next morning, we arrived at the courthouse confused and clearly out of our element. A maze of corridors, closed doors, and muffled conversations greeted us, but which direction would take us to the office for the state attorney? We turned a corner and bumped into the lawyer handling the prosecution. He would be our only voice in the whole matter. He was the Crown's prosecutor but stated very clearly that he would not be representing us. He was, however, our only access to the accused.

We were led to a cramped office where we sat like wooden statues in the small reception area. My statement was pried from my frozen fingers for photocopying. I glanced at the wall and noticed an assortment of pamphlets, and my eyes fastened on one that dealt with sudden death. I reached over, tugged one out, and tucked it in my purse. I hoped this would be the last time we ever set foot in this office.

Suddenly and without warning, we were told that the time to depart for the hearing was upon us. We were led to a stuffy room and told to have a seat, and then we waited again. No clocks adorned the walls, so it was left to my imagination the length of time that passed. Sometime later, we were told that the issue "had been called and stood down." Confusion registered on my face until it was explained that the court would take a break before it reconvened. Miraculously, my silent question as to the location of the accused received an answer. "Yes, the accused is in attendance." We did not see him, or maybe we did. We would not know him to recognize him unless, of course, he wore a sign on his back stating that he was the man who killed Corey Frenette. I needed to escape the closed room, if only for a little while, or else I felt sure I would faint. We walked to a nearby café and feigned hunger. I sat in a booth, my sweaty and nervous hands clasped tightly together, my stomach tied in knots as we waited for the cell phone to ring, summoning us back to the courthouse. When the call came, it jarred my raw nerves and sent my stomach plunging.

We arrived back at the courthouse to the announcement as it blared over the loudspeaker, "Courtroom 227 will now be reconvening." We hurried in. We managed to capture front-row seats as we sat cloistered together. We were told by Crown the cause for the delay—our Victim Impact Statements. The judge wanted to read them over thoroughly and carefully. We were told that each one received due consideration. When we asked if the defendant's lawyer read them, we were told he casually glanced at them before tossing them aside. We included a picture of our family with the statements, but this was returned to us. The defense did not feel the picture was relevant to the case. Heaven forbid that a face and a family were attached to the tragedy; it might prove too heavy a burden for the accused and his lawyer to carry. Far better to keep it as obscure as possible, remove the humanity of the situation by keeping the words brief and pictures out of sight.

I did, however, have an ace up my sleeve. I had grabbed Corey's graduation picture before leaving home. I proudly held it aloft for the judge to see. I was determined that if this was my only chance to put a face to the case number, then this is what I would do. I deduced that the man sitting directly behind the defense attorney was the man who killed Corey. I was astonished to find that this man, this killer, looked so ordinary. There were no telltale signs proclaiming what he had done to our lives. There was no branding burned into his cowardly skin. He was just a common human being who lacked a conscience. He stared straight ahead, and I wished I could read his thoughts. Was his cold-blooded heart jackhammering away inside his chest?

Our case was eighth on the list. The Crown stated its position and provided pictures to the judge, displaying the extent of the damage inflicted on Corey's car. He referred to our son by name as he tried to attach humanity to an impersonal proceeding. In a loud and clear voice, he stated, "His family is present in the courtroom." He attempted to instill some heart into the whole matter, but unfortunately, he had to stick to the facts, casting emotion aside. In summation, Crown asked for a fine of between $1,000 and $2,000. After concluding, the defense received equal opportunity to present its case. Upon opening, the accused was portrayed as a poor and broken man, a model citizen. Three letters of reference attesting to this man's fine and outstanding character were presented as evidence. Who dared to provide such endorsements on his behalf? Were they aware what actions they were defending? As the lawyer spoke, he reiterated that to this day, the accused was unable to say how the accident actually happened. All he knew was that a vehicle appeared outside his passenger side window.

The accused once owned a restaurant in Nanaimo but sold it after the accident and moved to Quebec. He was unable to work, existing on welfare. He divorced in 1996 and had no children. However, he was very proud to be retraining as a truck driver. I was appalled. If he could cause this much damage with four wheels, what could he do with eighteen? Heaven help the people on the highway. The defense asked that the court consider a fine less than the amount requested by Crown. Revoking his license was not a suggestion or even a consideration.

After listening to both sides, the judge nervously shuffled his papers, knowing what he was about to say would be inadequate given the dire circumstances and tragic consequences. He cleared his throat and began to speak. He began by acknowledging the nightmare in which we now found ourselves. As he prepared to deliver the sentence, he told the court that there were no mitigating factors—no alcohol was involved, and no record of previous driving charges was registered. The defendant had been on his way to buy supplies for his restaurant. As I listened, I felt the hope within me begin to die. No chance remained for retribution. When the judge announced his decision, even though I should have been, I was not prepared. "I hereby impose a fine of $1,500 to be paid in full by December 1, 1997. Case dismissed." With the pounding of the gavel, the legal proceedings ended. It was over, just like that. It was time for us to leave. As I gathered my belongings together, I realized I had been crying the whole time as I recalled the sheriff bringing me a box of tissue. We began to follow the coordinator of Victim Services out of the courtroom. Before we left, we stopped in our tracks, looking at the accused. I knew my husband well enough to know he would not allow this opportunity to slip through his fingers. A chance to confront this person would never happen again.

I watched as Tom approached him with Corey's picture in his hand. He extended it in front of the man who killed our son. "This is our son, Corey. Look at him."

The accused said, "I saw his picture in the paper. I am sorry, but I do not know how it happened." I listened as this person spoke, amazed that he continued to refuse to accept responsibility for his actions.

I glared at him and said, "That's my son. You killed my boy." If he would not voluntarily take the blame, then I was more than willing to give it to him. He could not look us in the eye. He nervously glanced at me then quickly looked away. He was a total and complete coward. He may have felt remorse; he may even have felt guilt. But he never admitted it. Maybe he felt very good about foiling justice and not having to own up to his actions. Maybe he felt very satisfied with himself. He duped everyone. But could he fool himself?

We left the courtroom, immediately ushered by the prosecutor and coordinator to an office where I noticed the sun as it streamed through the unadorned window. I am sure we were sequestered to avoid any further encounters with this man. They waited patiently as we composed ourselves. The prosecutor informed us that the press wished to speak with us, as Corey's young age had captured their interest. The thought kept reverberating around in my head—he only had to pay $1,500, while we had to pay for the rest of our lives. We continued to weep. They asked if we would like to say anything. The only thing that came to my mind was a simple thank you, for which I received a reply of, "You are welcome." I told the prosecutor that Corey thanked him as well. He said, "Corey is welcome."

The coordinator could not help but notice my anguish. She said, "Maybe you should let Corey go. Maybe by doing that, you will attain peace, and the torment will cease."

There was that phrase again. I looked her dead square in the eye and told her, "I let my son *go* in the hospital. I gave him permission to die. There will be no further 'letting go,' of this I am certain."

She believed Corey had to go to the next level. I contemplated what that meant. I had no control over Corey. It was not up to me to let him go. He could come and go as he pleased. That left me wondering what I was supposed to let go. I continued to ask that question again and again.

We returned Ally to school and hoped she would find a way to cope with the rest of the day. I suppose she felt like somewhat of a celebrity after attending a sentencing at a courthouse. I felt emotionally drained. No satisfaction was obtained, and there was no sense of closure. What was closure? I guess it meant that another part of our lives was over. *Closure* belonged in the same group as *getting over it* and *letting go*. Those nauseating, politically correct phrases meant nothing to me.

The next morning, we woke to hear the broadcast of our court case on the radio. It seemed strange to hear Corey spoken of in such a detached fashion. He was just a name on the radio, a victim of someone's careless driving, and the price tag attached to his life was insulting. Within a minute, the news flash ended, and the announcer moved on to other stories.

In a vain attempt to restore some semblance of normalcy to my life, I decided to go through one of our drawers and sort out some old clothes. And in that instant, I came across Corey's wallet. The night it was handed over to us flooded back to me. He lay in the hospital's emergency room, and a plastic bag containing his personal belongings was delivered to us. His last name was written in black marker across the front of it. His wallet lay among his socks and shoes. I instantly regressed to that moment in time when my world began to disintegrate. Instead of fighting it, I let it carry me over the edge. I cried my heart out.

Tom's sister called after our final encounter with the justice system. Tom relayed to her the punishment imposed by the courts. She was shocked and had thought that "this part" was over a long time ago. We immediately received an invitation to visit with her and her family. I was torn; I did not know how to connect with someone I thought I knew but found I no longer did. I decided to go as a support for Tom.

To say the visit was superficial and phony is to be kind. Tom brought up the subject of the sentencing, and she said, "I heard it on the radio." What was wrong with her? Here it was, on the radio, in full broadcast of his family, and news would surely have spread like wildfire. Yet not one of them picked up the phone to call and talk to him. Not one of them showed up or expressed regret for not attending with us that day. But neither were we chastised for not including them. Tom offered to leave copies of our Victim Impact Statements with her to read, and she accepted. I knew that when she finished reading them, they would be tucked away, forgotten in the back of a drawer until one day, she would unexpectedly come across them. The case, for her, was closed a long time ago. For us, it continued to go on and on.

After our frivolous visit, one of Tom's nieces called. She asked, "How are you?"

This question really grated on my nerves, so I shot back, "In what way?"

"In every way" was her reply. So I informed her how I was. She asked, "Are you seeing a counselor?"

I replied, "No."

"Do you have anyone to talk to?"

"No," I replied once again. "After a while, no one wants to hear about your emotional pain."

She asked, "What can I do for you?"

I said, "I don't know." I had become incapable of figuring out what I could do for me or what it was I needed. If I could not figure it out, how could I expect to pass that information along? She was the only relative I knew who displayed enough courage to actually go as far as she did. She, at least, made an honest attempt. Yet when I think of it now, sixteen years later, there is so much that can be done—not in regard to changing what happened but rather in learning how one person can make a difference.

When one stands on the outskirts gazing into another person's world, objective observation is relatively easy. To a certain extent, objective assessment means loss of humanity. For instance, I was told that Corey's death was inevitable, that it wasn't anyone's fault. That accident just happened to be the means by which Corey would die. She may have believed in fate and destiny, but did that mean she had the right to use my son as an example for her belief system? A very easy statement to deliver considering her child didn't die. Didn't she know this was the last thing I wanted to hear—a justification of my tragedy? By making such an inhumane comment, she effectively removed the blame from the person who caused the accident and conveniently placed it upon the shoulders of destiny.

Corey's accident and death consumed me. I watched for signs and waited in breathless anticipation for dreams. Visions of Corey were all I had left. How much longer could I hold on? What would happen if I let go? Songs that Corey loved stabbed me in the heart. His picture caused such pain in my soul that I shook as if I were chilled to the bone. I feared my spirit had vacated this earthly plane as well. All that remained was my body. I ached and yearned to be with him. My soul cried out for him. I felt completely and utterly lost.

Out of desperation, I sought the services of a psychic. Ever the skeptic, yet anxious to know more about the unseen world, I booked an appointment for the next day.

From the first moment I met this woman, I instantly became enveloped in a sense of warmth and love. She was a very amiable person who immediately made me feel comfortable and at ease. She prepared tea, and we chatted easily about anything and everything.

When I finished drinking, I followed her instruction on what to do with my empty teacup. She told me many things, but the most profound was her vision of seven people sitting around a table. One person sat with her back to me, hunched over and wearing a hat. She said that the body language indicated that the person in question was not in agreement with a decision we made. She told me when we travel, make sure we take care of ourselves, as we are in pain and perhaps not as attentive. She showed me the bottom of my teacup, and I immediately recognized the shape of Florida. We had been there nine months previous. When she rotated the cup, she said that we would be taking another trip. and when we travel, we do it because it is all we can do. She showed me our next destination, and I instantly recognized the Baja peninsula. We had just recently purchased our tickets for Mazatlan.

Then she proceeded to tell me that I was working on a project, something I kept close to me and few people knew about. She said it would help many people and prove to be very successful.

After she finished, we discussed what she had seen, and I began to fill her in on the details of my life. She returned to the question of the unidentified person with her back toward me, clearly in opposition to what I was doing. Who was this person with the hat? I couldn't figure out the answer to that question. Neither could I pinpoint the identities of the seven people who sat around a table.

It's funny how life's puzzles become solved mysteries. At the time, I had innocently participated in a conversation between two people who worked with me. As my administrator prepared to dash out the door to another all-important meeting, she said it was getting difficult to remember the role she played because she had so many hats to wear. I recalled many times approaching her regarding extended time off at Christmas; she would emphatically state her opposition to our time away. She felt it was her job to try to talk some sense into me, hunching over as she spoke, her body language speaking louder than her words.

I remembered all the conversations we had together in the quiet sanctuary of her office. It took very little coaxing for me to begin talking. If I received the slightest indication of interest regarding my personal life, the conversation would begin to flow, and with it the pent-up emotions gushed forth. She would bravely enter the off-limits waters and gently prod me into discussion. In retrospect, it seems she may have been using the opportunity to impose her logic on me. This might guide me back to a more sane and rational way of thinking. One time, she confided her belief in the afterlife and her conviction that people lingered after they died. She said that if you talked to them, they listened, for they were always within speaking distance. That was all the encouragement I needed to begin conversing about a topic I was very hesitant to bring up.

Believing I had found a confidant, I told her about the dreams I experienced almost on a nightly basis. After listening intently, she asked if my dreams were becoming more sporadic and further apart. I replied that they were unpredictable. I could not forecast when I would be visited or how long those visits would last. Her next statement erased whatever belief I had in her ability to appreciate my circumstances. "Maybe you are dreaming of him so much because you are reluctant to let him go."

I told her in a very matter-of-fact tone, "If that is the case, then I expect to continue to dream of him for the rest of my life."

Those dreams were my only chance to see him, an opportunity for us to reconnect after countless days apart. Why would I want them to stop? He understood my sorrow and heartache. And for that brief moment in time, the yearning would cease, as the parallel between life and death narrowed and merged. I cherished the times I spent with Corey as much as I enjoyed the time I spent with Corey's sisters. I always looked forward to the next time we would talk. Parents never let their children go. We can't. In the same breath, we can't hold them back either, so I suppose we compromise, meeting somewhere in the middle.

Chapter Fourteen

Rick

My mother-in-law once told me that no matter how many children a woman had, no two were alike. She spoke from experience, having borne thirteen of her own. But I found that she was wrong. Within her own brood, she did indeed have two that shared many similarities.

That unique bond was shared between Tom and his older brother Rick. Over the course of time and distance, they had drifted apart, as was natural among mature siblings. But Rick came back into our lives just when we needed him most.

It was the summer of 1997; four years had lapsed since the last time Tom and Rick spoke. Prior to that, thirteen years had slipped past with virtually no contact between them. But Tom never gave up on his brother. He knew in his heart that one day Rick would find the way back to him.

After suffering years of isolation and estrangement from his mother and siblings, Rick had a change in circumstances that provided him with the opportunity to make amends and seek forgiveness from his family. One of his first priorities was reaching out to Tom.

The last time Rick had spoken with Tom was on our trip back to Ontario in 1993. We had been camping, and Tom called Rick to ask if he would like to see us. Unfortunately, turmoil within his own family made it impossible for Rick to get together with us at that time. Tom expressed his regret while trying hard to understand the reasoning behind such a decision. Before hanging up, he told Rick we would always welcome him back into our lives.

I can't imagine the courage it took for Rick to pick up the phone, dial our number, and wait for someone to answer. The moment Tom found out who was calling, he did everything he could to let Rick know how much he missed hearing from his brother, and mostly that Rick was always and forever welcome in our home. Rick happened to be heading out our way from Ontario and wanted to know if he could stay for a couple of days.

After Tom told me about their conversation, I immediately began to agonize about the impending visit. What would be expected of us? Was this another relative who would require a performance from us? But I reminded myself that Rick was stepping onto our turf, and if we chose to speak of Corey that would be up to us. The biggest issue, by far, would be trust. Could we trust him?

I wanted to believe that Rick was the same person he was the day I first met him, possessing the biggest of hearts and always saying kind things about others, no matter the wrong they caused him. He taught Tom much in the ways of giving and receiving. Yet I remained unquestionably wary. I decided I would do my best to respect their time together and allow them the time and space they needed to connect again. A deep and nagging need existed for Tom to talk to someone, and Rick was just the ticket.

I believe that 1997 was a turning point for us. Missing Corey had not ended, for it never would, but I believed that Corey had sent his uncle to help in whatever way possible. Tom was very hesitant; he wasn't particularly looking forward to a lecture and the inevitable emotional bandaging that would be sure to follow. His sisters were notorious for that.

The night Rick arrived in town, we prepared ourselves as best we could. I was undeniably nervous as we drove to pick him up. Yet the moment I saw him, all misgivings instantly evaporated. It was as if we had never been apart. The first thing that struck me about Rick was his genuine warmth and caring. There was nothing pretentious about him at all. He was here with a very deep need as well. If he had any ulterior motives, he kept them very well hidden.

Upon our arrival back home, we seemed unsure of our next move. Where would we start? We decided to let our instincts guide us, and that first step led us to our backyard. This proved to be a definite icebreaker as we introduced Uncle Rick to Corey's garden. Rick became instantly captivated by all our efforts to create a special place in the world just for Corey.

After touring all the nooks and crannies, we headed inside and sat at the kitchen table overlooking our garden. Gazing out the patio window, Tom and I sat silently, drawing on the valuable art of listening. Rick began to tell us about his life, slowly painting a picture of the past ten years and the agony and suffering he had endured. His attitude toward his soon-to-be ex-wife was admirable, for he never spoke unkindly about her. We told him that we admired his strength in breaking free of the hold she had on him. He was quick to respond that he did not feel strong. He recognized the downhill slide his life was taking and knew he had to do something to reverse it. Instead of feeling strong, he said he felt thankful. Rick spoke openly for the next three hours, pouring out all the hurt and pain, but he would stop and check to see if we were okay with listening. The connection we had hoped for grew stronger by the minute.

The next morning marked the start of a very special day for all of us. The sun shone warmly, and I began to see the world through a different set of eyes. I felt like I was slowly awakening from a coma as I noticed and appreciated my surroundings. The five of us hiked to a restaurant for breakfast and then went shopping. When we returned home, we barely caught our breath before piling into the car to drive down to the waterfront.

Once we parked the car, we strolled along the seawall. As we passed the small, lighted towers that sat on the floating piers, I gave each of them a loving touch. They were as Corey had left them in the summer of 1994. I gazed at the paint splatters that decorated the boardwalk in a friendly freckled pattern. As Corey dipped his paintbrush, droplets fell off and collected on the weathered boards. They remained, but he had gone. And I knew one day those fixtures would require a new coat of paint. At that moment, another piece of Corey would vanish forever. Rick may have noticed the lingering caress as I walked, but without an explanation, he would not be able to understand the reason behind my actions. God, how I missed my boy.

It did not take long for me to recognize the precious gift presented to us. Instinct told me that Rick was the person who would save us. After less than twenty-four hours in his company, I found the world not as cold and lonely as it had been a week before.

Rick had been estranged from his own children for many years and missed them dearly. He felt so lost and alone. He didn't know if he could ever hope to repair all the damage that had been done. He had grandchildren he had never met and longed to know. He saw a whole different life abounding with endless possibilities, but he didn't know how to take the first step to get there.

That second night, we decided the time was ripe to introduce him to Corey. Tom brought the subject up by telling Rick he noticed the definite lack of reference made to Richard, his oldest son. Rick agreed that the rift of many years continued, but he thought perhaps because Richard was the eldest he suffered the most. A devout believer in Christ and His teachings, Rick prayed on a daily basis that somehow Richard would find it in his heart to forgive his dad so they could one day reconnect and enjoy life together. To this day, Rick continues to pray for the restoration of this broken relationship.

With this introduction to lost children, Rick seized the opportunity to ask about the delicate subject of Corey. Because we had not spoken Corey's name much except in the most casual of references since Rick's arrival, Rick began by saying that people were worried about us. I recognized the familiar tension building in Tom's jaw as he tightly clenched his teeth together. Rick acknowledged that we appeared to be okay, but he was uncertain what that actually meant. Our defenses immediately rose to the forefront and Tom quipped, "We're good actors." Once those floodgates were minutely cracked open, there was little hope of stemming the tide that would ultimately gush out.

We told him we were not angry; we were just people with so much to say and not one person who would listen. It was both a relief and a sorrow to share our feelings. We confided how we felt alone in wanting to preserve the very special love we held for Corey. We told him of the pressure we were subjected to as people told us to give that up, to let Corey go. We spoke of how terrifying it was to lose someone you love so dearly. He told us from his own personal experience to expect that the pain would never go away, to ignore what other people said or thought. We had to be true to ourselves.

Tom revealed to him how we were only maintaining what we had at the moment and by the end of the day, there was nothing left for anyone. That was the reason for us not calling or writing. I added that when I did write, it was completely taken out of context. I had to seek the delicate balance of expressing what I felt in a way that would not offend anyone, and that required more energy than I possessed.

We spoke of angels. We agreed there were some people who would say no such thing existed. But angels were everywhere, and when we needed one or ten, all we had to do was ask. They were right there waiting for us to call.

We stayed up until after 3:00 a.m., but it did not matter. The only thing of importance was that we were talking to someone and exchanging information and thoughts while gaining the valuable commodity of unconditional love and support.

We did not get much sleep that night. Rick would be leaving our home soon, and we did not want him to go. We knew silence and loneliness would fill the place where he had been. We were thankful for the time we had with him and appreciated the lack of outside interference during our time together. Rick was very quick to tell us that he had not come out here for other people; he came out for us. He knew we needed him, and he never thought twice about coming to us.

The following morning, we ate muffins and drank coffee on the patio. Tom disappeared for a while, and I took advantage of his absence to tell Rick something that had been nagging at me.

Time was of the essence, so I did not have the luxury of beating around the bush. I told him I would not allow him to hurt Tom, and that if he had any ideas of casually breezing into our lives and then abandoning us, he had better think twice. I told him that Tom needed him, but if he were to be tossed aside, I would never forgive Rick. But Rick assured me he was in our lives for the long haul, and he wanted to help us in whatever way he could. If it meant listening, then he would listen. He was not afraid of hearing the story of what we lived. He had no intention of trying to fix anything. The only personal item on his agenda was wanting to be here for us and our family. Without realizing it, I had been holding my breath, waiting in fearful anticipation that what I said would be misunderstood. What a relief I felt as I slowly exhaled and realized that I had not only made my point, but I had also not offended him in the process.

Because my husband had not yet returned, I decided to press further and give him a message almost twenty-two years late in its delivery. It concerned his first wife, Micky, who died suddenly and tragically on Christmas Day in 1975. I told him about a dream I had of her within a week of her death. Time passed without further contact from her, and I was not sure what I should do with the lingering memory of that one special dream. It rightfully belonged to Rick, and my role was solely as the messenger.

Micky had appeared before me in my sleep and said, "Tell Rick I am happy. Tell him I am okay." I remembered it so clearly. When I awoke, I felt so foolish for having such a dream and wondered why I had been chosen. Maybe she knew it would get through and therefore trusted me. As I divulged my long-kept secret to Rick on that bright summer morning, he became very contemplative, and a small smile tugged at the corners of his mouth. That smile was very reminiscent of the one Micky once wore. I told him that I relayed this same message about ten years earlier to his second wife and her advice was, "Forget it." I was warned not to be filling his head with such nonsense. She said it was in the past, and that was where it belonged. As a result, I had never told him until that moment.

As I waited for a response from him, my only wish was that I had not flubbed it. It was so wonderful when he finally responded with a simple, "Thank you." I had been able to give him something that we all hoped for, what we all longed to know, a sign that life had not entirely ended. Love endured and carried on. There really was a place where we would all connect again one day. Magnificent and wonderful people would be there, waiting for us to enter through heaven's gates. And the distance between heaven and earth was no further than a single step.

After Tom returned, I suggested that he and his brother go out and spend some time together. Tom and Rick returned a few hours later and with that arrival, Rick began to make preparations to leave. I openly wept as he stood in our driveway saying good-bye. When it came my turn to hug him, I clung to him, never wanting to let him go. I wished I could have found that magical potion that would postpone the inevitable. How ironic—in the beginning, we felt apprehension about seeing him and letting him in, but in the space of three days, he managed to rein in our hearts and soothe our fears.

One moment he was there, and the next he was gone. My heart left with him.

As the deafening silence settled like dust around the house, we thought about this visit with Rick and what it meant to us. I realized there was one thing this special man had done for me that no one else ever did. He taught me how to miss my son. He taught me it was okay to yearn for him and wrong for me to pretend otherwise. In an artificial world of make-believe and pretense, I was shown the path to my pain. This house had life. It was full. It was filled with people who loved and missed Corey.

Yes, Rick's visit was full of heartache, but interwoven were other real emotions—happiness, joy, and sorrow. We also shared anger. We shared companionship, anguish, forgiveness, and most importantly, love. Those were the ingredients that comprised life. Tom and I had both become so numb that we forgot what life was about. Too much emphasis had been placed on burying the past, of getting on with our lives, of moving forward, that we denied ourselves access to our true feelings. We buried those feelings, and if not for Rick, they may very well have been entombed forever. He gave us a glimpse of life. We were allowed to express our confusion over why our son died. We were given permission to say we missed Corey more than anyone would ever know. We were not chastised as we expressed our willingness to do anything to get him back, even though we knew in our hearts that was not possible. Our love for Corey was revealed in its true depth, and it was empowering to have it recognized and appreciated by someone else.

It seemed to me that society was only concerned with one thing, and that was the act of healing. Mourning in public was discouraged, as I quickly found out. If I did not at least give the impression that I was healing, I was bombarded with suggestions designed to send me down the road to recovery. So instead, I turned inward. I embraced nature, where I found Corey's presence most prevalent. He sang to me while whispering my name in the breeze. He embraced me, resulting in the feeling of warm chills. I knew he was near even though I could not see him, and I believed in his undying existence. And it took the magic of Rick to show me what I had known in my heart all along.

A few days after Rick left for home, Tom, Ally, and I decided to go camping on Newcastle Island, which was accessible only by a small foot-passenger ferry. No motorized vehicles were allowed, although bicycles were permitted.

After setting up camp, we embarked on our customary hike around the island. A complete circumnavigation took two or three hours, depending on the length of the stride and the chosen path. We strolled along the pebble beach, and when it became too difficult to traverse, I headed off independently to search for a more favorable path. As my family's voices faded, memories of Corey quickly took up residence in the quiet space of my mind. On more than one occasion, Corey had brought his bike here and ridden the trails while we tagged along behind him. I could picture him as he rode over the roots and rocks that littered the pathway. The trees would cast dappled shadows on his head and when the sun broke through the canopy overhead, his hair would glisten with the captured rays reflecting gold and red amongst the curls of brown. On the trail that warm summer day, he was right in front of me, riding as he used to so long ago. My eyes filled with tears, and my heart ached to see him again.

From my vantage point, I caught glimpses of Tom and Ally as they made their way across the lichen-covered rocks, carefully avoiding the pitfalls along the way. Suddenly, a raven appeared in the towering cedars above me, calling down a greeting. I sobbed when I noticed its presence and instantly linked the bird to the spirit of Corey. As I continued my trek through the forest, the raven caught flight, flew ahead of me, and landed softly in a fir tree not far away.

It watched me as I plodded along, cawing to me in encouragement from above. When I drew near to the area where it waited, I noticed as once again it flew off and landed in another tree not too far in the distance. It repeated this pattern several times until the moment Tom and Ally converged with me on the trail. When I pointed out the bird that walked with me, it had vanished. Tom quickly assured me he knew Corey watched over me, calling to me as he guided me along, making sure I was not alone.

While walking that stretch of path with only the bird as my companion, my thoughts wandered as I reflected on how out of touch I felt, how unfocused and lost my life had become. I wondered what was to become of me. I felt useless and unworthy. Life should be reserved for those who have much to give, who cherish and respect it, who value its precious gift. I envied those around me who were complete, who felt joy, who loved without fear of losing it all in a heartbeat. I envied today what I had yesterday.

I thought about the other side of life, the side where Corey now lived. Where was he, and what did he do during what we knew as days? When I became overwhelmed, I would retreat to the sanctuary of my backyard. Did Corey's world ever overwhelm him? Where was his haven? Did he have one? Was he able to retreat? Did he have the luxury of relaxing? What was his world like? I could not imagine life without Corey, yet here I was, living it. I hated it, yet I was still here. Why?

I felt trapped between two worlds. In this one, my body and mind existed. Tom and the kids needed me. Feelings of guilt would wash over me when I realized I was living here without Corey, and I would question that if my kids needed me on this plane, didn't Corey need me where he was? Or when a child died, did they automatically become independent and not need their parents anymore? Did he yearn for me as I yearned for him? I knew when I died, the yearning for Corey would cease, and the pain of his death would vanish. Perhaps for the ones left behind, they would take up the torch of yearning, and the pain of my death would become theirs to bear. Right now though, I would give anything for one more moment with Corey. Death was always hardest on those left behind.

Among the many things I lost, I missed the unrestrained, rushing-headlong-into-life-without-a-care-in-the-world feeling. I profoundly distrusted life. I thought about Corey's sisters carrying such sadness in their lives, but I hoped that despite wearing the scar of grief, maybe they would somehow regain that feeling of trusting life, embracing life and all the joys it had to offer.

I thought about all the experiences Corey would miss. There would be no sharing the excitement of a new truck in the driveway, having quiet conversations about the new love of his life, watching him pack up all his belongings and helping him settle into his first apartment, picking up the phone and talking to him for no particular reason other than to say hello and hear his voice. When I thought of what could have been, it cut me to the quick. Reminders and thoughts of what could have been were everywhere.

I had grown enough to realize that caution was the way for me to proceed through life. I did not know how to reach out to someone else. Why would I choose to impose my pain on another? Why would anyone in their right mind want anything to do with the enormous hurt that had become such an all-consuming part of my life? How does one break down that barrier? How does someone get past that wall? I quickly found the answer to those questions. In order to achieve that, two people have to be very determined, very willing to go where no one else dares to go, take that first step, and say, "Please tell me what is on your mind. I really want to know how it is that you manage on a day-to-day basis." It could be two strangers united in grief, lonely people on the same path. Believe it or not, people who are not on the same path but dare to join another, if only for a little while, actually exist, although they are very rare. Bereaved parents need only look around to see the truth behind this statement.

I am fortunate to have a friend like that. My friendship with Allison stretches back thirty years. Tom and I met Allison and Ken through the school our children attended. Their daughter Kate spent thirteen years with Corey in the same schools, and they graduated together. Kate knew Corey, but never as more than a casual acquaintance. My friendship with Allison started out as a seed, and over the years, it grew and flourished. Allison possessed a certain magical quality that made me feel as if I were her only friend when in truth, she had many. She was a warm and genuine person, kind and gentle.

When our children left elementary school and entered high school, we lost touch. I guess we had gone our separate ways. I worked outside of the home while she devoted her time to volunteering, helping other people, and nurturing her family. She also dedicated a great deal of time to her true passion—gardening.

When Corey died, the separate forks of our lives suddenly merged and became one. Since that time, we have become inseparable.

I vaguely recall inviting Ken and Allison to our house for a quiet talk. The initial throngs of support had receded, but the burning desire to pour out my feelings smoldered hot and true. As we sat together, Tom and I spewed forth our story, and they listened intently and uttered not a word. Tom told them things he had never told another soul except me. This cascading of emotion taxed his precious reserve of energy.

When we were emotionally spent, they asked questions in a further attempt to try to understand. As they prepared to leave that night, I suddenly turned to Allison and asked if perhaps we could resume our friendship. As she warmly embraced me, she told me she was going to ask the same thing of me.

True to her word, Allison invited us to their home for an evening of companionship and card-playing. We were in their living room, and I sat near the hearth of the fireplace. We were speaking of things in general when I happened to glance down at the floor. A book lay on the carpet beside me, so I picked it up. I have heard that people don't choose books but rather books choose people. I looked at the cover, noticing that the author had a particularly sad quality about her. Although she was smiling, the smile failed to extend past her lips. Her eyes deeply reflected emotional pain. I turned the book over to read what it was about. I heard Allison shuffle uneasily in her chair, perhaps wishing she hadn't left that book lying around.

I couldn't understand what the book was about, so I asked.

"Well, it's something I picked up while I was at the library," Allison said. "I was hoping to gain a little insight into what it is you are feeling. It's written by a woman who lost her son, and this is her story."

Instantly intrigued, I asked if I could borrow it after she was done with it. As I flipped through the pages, words began to leap out at me. "Brain death," "life spirit," "shock," "disbelief," "horror," and "life support." Melody Beattie wrote a book about her own life experience, detailing events that chillingly paralleled my own. *Lessons of Love* came an inspiration to me as well as a guide that continually conveyed the message, "You are not alone." I don't know how many times I read that book, but each time it felt like the first. With each reading, I learned a little more about coping, hanging on, and believing when the people around me stopped believing.

Allison has never asked me how I am. I told her at the outset that this question—"how are you?"—bothered me. People ask the question without real and true thought. I was expected to say I was fine when in fact, I was not. Allison nurtured my broken spirit, asking questions no one else would think to ask. She included Corey in all our conversations, and it's very clear and obvious that she has not forgotten him. And like Rick, she has found a special place in my heart.

Since that time, Allison and I have spent countless hours together. She has asked questions, validated my feelings, and never been ashamed to sit with me and cry. A friendship like ours is impossible to weigh, measure, or gauge. One in a million? One in a billion? It is as vast as the love from which it stems. She never patronized me or felt the need to fix me up. She allowed me to be myself, willingly venturing into the unpopular waters of grief and standing by, always at the ready, lest I slip beneath the waves and simply drown in sorrow.

Chapter Fifteen

Commitment

Beyond my kitchen window lays a potpourri of garden beds and hanging baskets. Every year, I plant assorted varieties and colors of annuals, work that takes me weeks to complete. As summer begins to wane and autumn advances, the demise of these plants is inevitable. Despite the nighttime temperature dipping ever lower, the hardy cosmos in particular will continue to flower and bloom, long after all the others have succumbed to the cold. I caught sight of a cluster of snowy white blossoms while I stood gazing out the window. My mind wandered, and as always, my thoughts included Corey. I noticed as a group of flowers began to sway back and forth, almost as if they were waving to me. The flowers surrounding them were silently still. I looked up at the trees and hanging baskets in the yard and saw no evidence of wind causing a noticeable stir. Even the outdoor chimes hung quietly. I glanced back, and the plant kept fluidly moving from side to side while, on the radio in the background, four songs played back to back, all with the same sad theme: "I will always be there." Hypnotized by what was happening around me, I immediately understood the message being conveyed to me. Corey was saying hello in the way only a parent would understand. As suddenly as they had begun their liquid movement, the flowers stopped, having filled me with hope and assurance that there was more to life than met the eye.

I made a commitment to myself involving the search for more information on Corey's medical condition after he was rushed to the hospital's emergency room. There was no logic to my quest. I simply had to know. In order for me to access whatever information was available, I would need to broach the subject with our family doctor. I made an appointment, which was the easy part. Telling him what I wanted would be an entirely different matter.

As I sat in the waiting area, I tried to think of a way to raise the subject that would lead to the real purpose of my visit. I decided to approach it by asking him if a person's medical records were destroyed within a certain time period following death or kept indefinitely. I felt I had every right to have the records as I continued trying to make sense of it all. Unfortunately, the medical profession did not see it from my maternal point of view. My doctor was less than pleased to hear about my ongoing obsession, as he called it, especially since he felt he had given me all I needed to know during the first month following Corey's death. If I had any illusions about how easy securing Corey's medical records was going to be, I learned quite the opposite during those ten minutes. But really, what else could I have expected? The doctor was a medical professional and assumed he knew the best avenue of treatment for me. Nevertheless, I told him that a few vitally important pieces were missing, such as the report from the local hospital. He told me I did not seem able to focus on reality, that I needed therapy.

Unbeknownst to him, I had acquired a few valuable skills. I knew all I had to do was tell him what he wanted to hear. As I sat there listening to his analysis of my needs, he asked me if perhaps I should contemplate his esteemed advice in regard to seeking professional help. My only wish was to secure the hospital records and be on my way. I told him I was considering it, even though it was the farthest thing from my mind. I knew what I needed and what I could do without. I attempted to explain to him what I was feeling, but I could see my words and logic fell upon deaf ears. He asked me if I was suicidal. This did not shock me, for I knew his thoughts. I said, "No, but there are those times when I lay down and can do nothing else." I told him all I wanted was for the emotional pain to stop. With prey in easy sight, he pounced with the question, "Are you ready for drug therapy?" Again, to appease his mind, I told him that I was considering this. If he knew me at all, he would have known that drug therapy was simply not worthy of debate. He assured me that the drug he had in mind was not a tranquilizer but rather a form of Prozac. The warning bells immediately sounded in my head. I had heard enough about Prozac to know what it was about, if only a little. He said it was nonaddictive with no side effects. I nodded, agreed, and tried to appear interested, all the while gazing at the reports safely tucked beneath his elbow. If only I could reach over, grab them, and run for the door. Carefully, I proceeded one step at a time. He told me I would probably only need two sessions of therapy to make me feel better. He asked me if I read any books. I admitted I had. He told me that if they could stick a tiny probe inside my head (no thanks!), a chemical imbalance would register and once that was corrected, he assured me I would be on the road to recovery. Would my son's death become easier to accept if I felt better? Would the blush on the rose of life return to its former glory? What about after the medication was withdrawn—or would I somehow learn how to feel better on my own and no longer need any artificial persuaders?

He informed me that I was depressed. I admitted that yes, I could see that I was depressed over the death of my son. I silently began to formulate the best answer I could possibly dream up in order to put an end to this meaningless banter destined to go nowhere. "Well, you have certainly given me a lot to think about. I will let you know what I decide." This seemed to satisfy his burning need to straighten me out, and he handed me the reports on my son. I managed to escape the office with my precious cargo tucked safely in my purse. I felt like a thief in the night. Why was I treated this way? After all, Corey was my child. Did I not have a right to know everything about his condition?

Upon my arrival back home, I carefully scrutinized the few pieces of paper. They contained information I had not been privy to before. For example, I found out that Corey's femur protruded from his leg by a full six inches. What sort of force would cause this to happen? It must have been a horrible sight to see. I imagined the pain would have been unbearable. Coupled with the severity of his head injury, it was beyond my ability to grasp the magnitude of what happened that night. According to the reports, he was unconscious but able to maintain his bodily functions. The effects of the trauma to his brain were not evident at the beginning. That horror would surface later. Yet the question needed to be asked—if he had received the CAT scan at the Nanaimo Hospital, would he have survived? If he had been transferred earlier, would he have lived? Although I never received an answer to either question, I could only conclude from what I read that his death was inevitable.

Why did I do this to myself? Why did I persist in exhuming this stuff that was best left in the past? The only answer was this: he was my child, and I had to know.

I searched for answers to questions I had not begun to ask. I tried to find out what happened to Corey, and was there any way he could have been saved. Did we make the right decision to discontinue his life support? Was there ever any hope? Did we prolong his suffering? At what point would he have died naturally? Did he needlessly suffer because of our own selfish needs?

That evening, as Tom and I sat at the kitchen table going over the information, the timer controlling the bank of lights over my plants spontaneously shut down. It was on that day, October 4, 1997, that Corey moved back home.

As we sat in the dark, we noticed the light closest to Corey's passionflower as it kept flashing. Tom instantly became fascinated with this strange phenomenon. He explained to me that when the timer shut off, all power was disconnected to the fixture. The circuit became interrupted and therefore incomplete. I called each of the kids down to see this, and their reaction was the same: "Corey?" Tom and I remained at the table and watched the light flash on and off for over an hour. As it continued to pulsate, the intensity began to diminish. Tom placed his hand near the light, and when he did, it instantly flared back to life. When he removed it, the light settled back down.

At that moment, Cleo began acting strangely. She meowed incessantly until I finally relented and followed her. She walked to Ally's chair at the kitchen table and gazed at the flickering light, meowing. She jumped up, meowed, and kept making a motion toward the blinking light. It was as if she wanted to get closer to it. As

I scooped her up in my arms and walked her closer to the light, she reached out, pawing at the empty air.

It seemed strange to think a flickering light could provide such comfort to us. But in my heart, I knew this was Corey's way of reaching out across the abyss that separates life from death. I also knew one day, the light would cease its dance, but that day was not today. I gathered this small reassurance to me and wrapped myself snugly in its consoling embrace.

Corey's birthday inched closer once again. I remained desperately lonely as I tried to think of a way to reconnect to society. When death decided to step into my life, any semblance to a normal existence disappeared. Three years after my son's life ended, I had lost all contact with members of our families. Friends, too, had long since scattered. With isolation as my only other option, I tentatively reached out to the only lifeline available—Compassionate Friends, a support group consisting entirely of parents whose children have died. There were no doctors, psychiatrists, or psychologists attending, just parents experiencing the same desolation, isolation, and loneliness that only we knew. When Eleanor, the esteemed leader of this group, answered her phone, she asked if I was Corey's mom, for she had been expecting my call. I admitted that I was, wondering why she would expect me to call. It could be that, unlike myself, she never gave up on me. Eleanor existed in the same ocean of grief as I did—she was someone who understood and did not judge. She felt like a breath of fresh air. It would be another three months before we, as Corey's parents, could attend a Compassionate Friends meeting.

During my initial contact with Eleanor, she told me I was not depressed, I was profoundly sad. That described exactly how I felt: saturated in sadness. Grief invaded every pore of my body, and no matter how hard I tried to occupy my mind or how busy I kept my hands, it was always there. I could not shake it, and I could not lose it. Like a shadow, it was attached to me.

Eleanor warned me that the relentless march of time would cause resentment. This was an enormous relief for me, because I thought I was in some way abnormal for hating the movement of time. Ultimately, all I really wanted was for my child to return. I wanted my life to be normal again. I wanted to share in all the joy life had to offer and not have those lingering thoughts of "if only Corey was here."

Eleanor confided that she often thought of calling, but knew I would one day call her on my own. She felt I had much to give. I could barely give to my own family and myself. How could I possibly have anything left to give to other people? She assured me that family members were scared, because we represented death. They wanted desperately to fix us. They did not know what to say or do. They chose instead to wait on the sidelines while we struggled.

When Eleanor mentioned that she had read Corey's tribute in the paper, saying we spoke the truth, she empowered me as we stated to the world what lay in our hearts. We needed to say it, and society needed to hear it. After my first tentative meeting with Eleanor, she contacted me every month asking if we were ready to join her group of bereaved parents. I always told her, "Not yet."

Grief dictated my life, and I no longer had any choice. I found that I would have very good intentions to do a certain task, but moments later, my pledge melted like ice cream on a hot summer day. Resolving myself to a project was the easy part. Commitment, the glue binding resolve together, was much more difficult. Sometimes it became necessary to give up so that I could gather my strength in preparation for the next heavy step.

I was scared. If I could no longer function around normal people, would I fail when placed in the midst of others who were just like me? What if I were the only woman abandoned and cast aside? How did other parents of children who died find the resolve necessary to go one more day, knowing that at the end of that day, their son or daughter would not be any closer to coming back home? What was this organization called Compassionate Friends all about anyway? Would they be there for us, to listen to us, to our story, to our pain, to our hearts, to our anguish? Would they judge us? Were we in any way different from them?

Every month when the day for the meeting arrived, I could never make a decision. Go or stay? Help or hide? That particular month, though, Tom arrived home late from work, and at 5:30 p.m.

I bargained with Corey: if his dad came home soon, it meant we were to attend. If he came later, that meant we were not supposed to go. Almost instantly, Tom pulled into the driveway and walked into the house, unaware that anything was amiss. The mental battle ended.

I chose to move to the next rung on the ladder of indecision. I resolved that I would take my cue from Tom. I knew it had been a rough day for him, and as we embraced, I asked him if he would like to go to a meeting. Without hesitation, he said, "Sure." He obviously experienced no problem with his own level of comfort. I was different. I needed to feel comfortable with the idea. That day, I felt okay in my decision.

There were not many people in attendance that evening. Upon entering the room, I gazed at all the people sitting around, amiably chatting. Had I walked into the wrong room? These people looked so normal. How was that for judging? As we sat down and looked at the other parents, I began to see their pain. They appeared normal, just as I did. They were able to converse and carry on, but there was obviously something hiding beneath the thin veneer, for the reminder of death was never far away. These parents wore their wounds on the inside.

It took great courage to expose my soul that night to people I had never met before. The initial idea of spending two hours in their company overwhelmed me, to say the least. What would we talk about? How were we going to connect? What would we say? Only after each one spoke of his or her own personal tragedy did it become evident that we all had something in common—our children were all dead. The world remained ignorant of our pain for the simple reason that it could not be seen. We did not carry our dead children around on our sleeves or have them hanging off our arms like bangles. The world could not tell by looking in our eyes or by deciphering the lines of grief etched deeply into our faces. Within moments of sitting down with this roomful of strangers, I realized that in my struggle to keep it all together, I had failed. It was nothing more than a facade. The surrealism and disjointedness were never far away. When grief began to close in, I realized nature protected me from what I could not absorb.

As Tom and I took turns speaking, we received affirmation from this small group of grievers that society viewed death as an inconvenience. Anger bloomed in that room along with a host of other undefined emotions. Yet it felt safe to express our feelings far removed from the rest of the world. Until that moment, I never realized how alone I was. I was trying to fit into my old life with a new and undefined shape.

During the meeting, stories of visits from deceased children surfaced. It was comforting for me to hear that other people experienced the exact same things. It encouraged me to know that no matter how much time passed, our children continued to visit us. I no longer needed to fear losing contact with Corey. He would always be there for his family.

As the end of the meeting approached, I found I did not want to leave. I felt closer to this small group of people than I did to my own relatives. These were parents in pain, afraid of the same sense of judgment. They expressed all the same doubts, hopes, fears, all the same wishes, all the same shattered dreams that followed death. They too suffered life with broken hearts. The bottomless depths of despair yawned widely and gaped at us as we struggled with fear in our vain attempt to comprehend the unimaginable. What if we never hit bottom? What if we did? I found grief to be riddled with countless false bottoms. Just when I thought I was as low as I could go, I would sink even further. With no one around to pull me back up, I had to claw and scratch my way to the surface, not knowing why I did.

At the close of the meeting, Eleanor warned me that the next several days could prove unbearable. Like freshly tilled soil, emotions had been unearthed and brought to the surface. The question regarding the wisdom of attending such a group would definitely rear its head.

True to her words, the next day was filled with incredible pain. I felt I could howl the whole day long as a deep overpowering need consumed me. I felt mortally wounded. I spent the better part of my morning curled up in bed. Finally exhausted, I pulled myself up and got dressed.

I took a walk in the fresh air, attempting to clear my mind and arrange my thoughts in order. As I walked that morning, the seed for *Lost in Grief* began to take root. If I had one thing to communicate to people, what would it be? The answer was simple: be there. Do not run, but rather be brave and stay with those who grieve.

I believed that everyone we knew was affected by Corey's death, but they stood safely on the outskirts, looking in. In time, they would turn away forever. In the interim, they waited for the magical words that would restore everyone's lives, as if I were directly responsible for the disruption. "Ah, there. I feel so much better. I am now healed and would like to be a part of your life again." The sad part was I would never be able to say those words. I would never again be all better.

Later that spring, my mother died, and with her death, many memories of my childhood surfaced. By far, the most painful memory involved her casual use of alcohol and Valium and the effect that had on us as children. When I turned seventeen, I ran away from home. Unable to stand her domineering personality for another moment, I packed a small suitcase and, with the aid of a school friend, fled into the cold winter night. I caught the first bus heading east and left the unenviable task of informing my mother to my friend. I also asked my friend to place a call to Tom, who was attending school in Toronto at the time. My plan was to go there to be with him. I ran to the only safe haven I knew—to the man who would shortly thereafter become my husband.

After I was informed of my mother's death, I knew I would not be attending her funeral. My older brother Garry opted to put in an appearance as a representative of her children. He told me I had enough to endure, and for the first time in a very long time, I felt he was behaving as an older brother should toward his younger sister.

Later that afternoon, as I was tending to my houseplants, I noticed the pulsating light was strangely silent and still. Despair flooded into my heart with the thought that Corey was now gone. The cold glass of the bulb no longer flared when I brought my hand close to it. Had he ever indeed been here? I never realized how comforting, how less alone I felt until that moment when the light ceased its erratic flashing dance.

Two days after Mom's funeral, I started noticing strange occurrences. The first involved the portable phone. It let out a loud "Bleat!" while resting in its cradle. Following a power outage, the plant timer assumed control of itself even after I tried resetting it. I noticed a burned-out lightbulb at the opposite end of the track, so I changed it out. As I slowly and carefully tightened it into place, imagine my surprise when it began flashing all on its own. Dare I hope? I looked to my right to see if the one powered by Corey had resumed its strobe-like dance. My heart filled with joy as the gentle rhythm of that flashing light reflected throughout the room. I excitedly pointed it out to Tom, and he said that Corey was back and had brought his grandmother with him. Perhaps he left us to help her adjust to her new world and thought to bring her back to our house.

My brother Garry called me after he returned from the funeral, and I could hear the sadness in his voice. He had always been a very practical person who rationalized everything in life. But he admitted to me that he could not make sense out of mom's death, except to say that perhaps she was no longer in pain. His struggle came with the natural desire to know what was next. Where had his mom gone?

Garry's mind rapidly filled with all these new, never-asked-before questions. I had tried many times to talk to him about the afterlife, but he was not receptive. Suddenly he had a reason to question and thus began his search for evidence that life did not end with physical death. He told me of a spiritualist/medium who had written a book entitled *Talking to Heaven* about experiences connected with people who were no longer of this earth. James Van Praagh relayed intimate details regarding the person who died, circumstances that he could not possibly know about. I had been telling Garry about Corey's energy, and I was amazed to hear him tell me that I should believe without question. He thought that maybe, just maybe there was something to it. I, on the other hand, had always known. He went on to tell me that people who died suddenly attached themselves to the living, because they could not adjust and therefore needed us to help them. I had always said that Corey helped us, and we helped him. His death was such a shock to him that it seemed only natural that he should reach out to his family. He knew we would never do anything to push him away.

I began reading *Talking to Heaven*. I had to order it special, but once I put my hands on it, I could not set it down. There were many instances of afterlife encounters, and I was fascinated with all that had been written. James talked about the different ways in which spirits communicate with us and stated, to my astonishment, that electricity was their favorite means, followed by television sets.

I went on to read the passage written about spirits presenting us with gifts. This brought numerous incidents to mind. By far, my most stunning gift from Corey was a ring I found on our visit to Maui in 1995.

While in Hawaii, we decided to check out a flea market that was held on Saturdays. Our tour book highly recommended it, and we thought it would be a worthy investment of our time. Exotic plants and flowers lined the walkways, and local fruits and vegetable were piled high on display. As a regular practice, we always sought out fresh vegetables for our meals, and this venture definitely proved to be worthwhile. As we continued our meanderings, we came across a table with a wide assortment of jewelry and cameras for sale. I do not know what captivated me about the ring, but I found it unusual in its simplicity and design. I certainly did not need another ring. I was, however, looking for something special as a reminder of Maui. I tried on the ring and admired it. The price was reasonable, but I could not justify spending that amount of money when we were only three days into our trip.

We returned to the flea market the following Saturday after I had spent the week agonizing over whether or not I should purchase the ring. I made a deal with myself: if I could find that ring again, I would buy it. Otherwise, if I were unable to relocate it, that would mean it was not destined to be mine.

We began searching for that same display but were unable to locate it. Was this a bad sign, or was this a challenge? I kept hunting.

After marching up and down every aisle and circumnavigating the perimeter, we finally achieved success.

I was immediately drawn back to the ring, mesmerized by its beauty. I tried it on again and told the lady it was very pretty. She graciously admired it on my hand. It quietly sparkled in the sunshine while begging, "Please buy me." I asked the price, and it was miraculously lower than a week ago. We chatted for a while as Tom perused the selection of used 35mm cameras. Our camera had jammed on us, and he was looking for another, either as a replacement or for spare parts. His eyes came to rest on an identical model. I looked longingly at the ring as Tom cradled the camera to his chest. We agreed to buy the camera and the ring together, but the price had to be right. The negotiation stage was about to begin; the players were all assembled as we waited in eager anticipation for the first bid to be announced. After a bit of wheeling and dealing, a compromise was reached. The ring was mine. The only thing I knew about my new piece of jewelry was the name of the three large stones. They were tourmalines with diamonds encircling each of them. The history and origin of tourmaline was a mystery I longed to uncover.

Months later, I took my ring to the jewelry store for an appraisal, asking the saleslady if she knew anything about tourmaline. Was it a semiprecious stone? Did it have any intrinsic value? She thought maybe the middle stone could be an emerald. I knew better than to raise my expectations to such unrealistic levels, simply because the couple in Maui knew their gems and certainly would not sell an emerald at such a low price.

After leaving my ring with the gemologist, I went home and began to search out information on tourmaline. I found it originated in the state of Colombia in South America. The next sentence stopped me in my tracks. Tourmaline was the birthstone for the month of October, the month of Corey's birthday, the same month I was in.

A week later, I picked up my ring from the jewelry store. I was astounded to learn it was valued at four times the amount which I had paid. The stones were indeed tourmaline. This was, without a doubt, a gift from Corey and as such, I would treasure it forever.

There could be no coincidence that diamonds were my birthstone. My son and I were bound together, and I had the ring to prove it.

Tom experienced a very strange occurrence during this time. I paged him at work and asked that he return my call. He phoned me on his cell phone and just as we began to talk, I had to put him on hold while I answered another call. When I returned to him, he said he would have to call me back. When he did, he arranged to meet me for lunch. After he picked me up, he made sure all the radios and electronic equipment were turned off. The only thing he left on was his pager. Then he proceeded to tell me his story.

"While I was waiting for you to come back on the line, I began to blow softly into the phone. Suddenly, I could hear myself over my mobile radio. When I moved closer to the radio, I received feedback. That meant I was broadcasting over the open air. But that couldn't be right, because the cell phone and the radio operate at two entirely different frequencies." When I asked him what the two frequencies were, he said, "One operates at 50MHz and the other is at 900MHz. They are incapable of crossing over, yet they did. So you tell me how that happened."

All these signs, signals, and efforts at communication offered immeasurable comfort but could not substitute for the day-to-day interaction with a live human being. And that made me angry. Anger would flare for no apparent reason. It didn't need a reason—it rode so close to the surface of my emotions that anger often governed all rational thought.

In 1998, summer arrived early, and we were well into our fourth month of hot, dry weather. Every day dawned cloudless, with endless wall-to-wall crystal-clear skies. I had recently completed the first draft of my manuscript and proceeded to work on the outline. The weather was so warm, the kids and I often packed up and headed to the beach for a few hours of respite. I would work on *Lost in Grief*, and the girls would splash in the ocean. This became our routine.

Tom unexpectedly came home in the middle of the week. I was in the midst of watering my baskets and garden beds, not paying much attention to what he was doing. It was not unusual for him to stop by and pick something up on his way to a job.

Suddenly and without warning, my eye caught sight of a large yellow object. Our neighbor's voice boomed and reverberated through our yard. I could not make the connection. I watched in abject horror as he and Tom lowered a massive yellow canopy in our backyard, resting it against the fence. My jaw dropped to the ground as I tried in vain to grasp the reasoning behind such an action. The only thing that came to mind was, "What in God's name is this canopy doing in my backyard?" Not very original, I know. It was monstrous, rising to a height of four feet while measuring over forty feet in length. The sun reflected off the canvas and slapped me in the face. I was beyond speechlessness; I was livid. I could feel my grip on tightly reined emotions collapse as I fought back fear, pain, tears, and anger. I became a runaway train on a steep downward slope, and straight ahead lay a ninety degree bend. The cable on the brake line of sensibility snapped.

I felt the rage building as I stormed from the backyard. Tom was inside his truck pulling out other strange paraphernalia for storage. Unfortunately, our neighbor was well within earshot as I hissed like a snake, "What the hell is that thing doing in our yard?" I detested hearing those words as they escaped from the depths of my soul, but I was well beyond reason. Tom sensed the rage directed at him and wisely chose not to answer me. This further inflamed me, and I repeated the question. I was on the verge of tears, so great was my frustration. Still Tom remained silent, but to my surprise, I received a reply.

A voice thundered and bellowed, "Ask no questions, Karen, and he will tell you no lies."

Great, just what I needed to hear. I could have ripped his throat out. I knew I was totally irrational, and Tom knew that nothing he could say would safely extinguish the flames of anger. He finished what he was doing and left without a word. Not long after the sound of his van faded, I came to the realization that there was just "it" and me. The sun beat down brightly on that yellow canvas beast and seemed to mockingly sneer at me as if to say, "So what are *you* going to do about it?" What *could* I do about it? I wanted to lift and throw it out of our yard, but its weight was too great. If

I could have, I would have dragged it screeching in protest across the pavement to the curb and deposited it in the middle of the street. But I could not lift a corner of this prehistoric reptilian canvas caterpillar. I closed my eyes and willed it to be gone. When I dared to peek again, it had not moved. Tears coursed down my face as I realized I could do nothing. I knew I could not stay another moment in the same yard with that gigantic immovable snakelike object leering at me as it sat against the fence, quite content with its new home. One of us would have to leave. I packed up a few things and headed to the beach. As I left our yard, I glared at it, wishing it would evaporate into thin air, knowing full well that it would still be there upon my return.

During my escape, I managed to slough off my anger. It flowed from my body as if the dam that was responsible for holding it all in had suddenly collapsed. I forgot about the yellow canopy as I submerged my soul in the peacefulness and tranquility of the ocean moment.

As I sat and thought about my reaction to an object made of canvas and steel, I wondered how it managed to elicit such a violent response from me. I was unable to accurately place my finger upon the reason for such an irrational reaction. I thought I had learned all the tricks and secrets to keeping my emotions safely in check and tucked away. I thought I was beyond provocation. I was, instead, just beginning to learn about the power of pain and grief. I had, until that point, believed all the material I had been given to read about how this was a one-shot deal, and when it was over, it was gone for good. I was ill-prepared for the wave of hostility as it sunk its poisonous fangs deep into my soul and spewed its toxic venom into every crevice, pore, and fissure of my being. The reason for my anger lay days away, and it would be months before I could fully understand and appreciate the level at which anger dwelled.

Upon returning home later that day, I saw the canopy as it had been left. Its position had not changed, and I had to face the fact that this was a reality. I then began the act of banishment. I refused to acknowledge its existence and sought to remove any visual contact with it from my field of vision. When I had to walk past it, I shielded my eyes from its hateful scowl. I could not budge it, but I could refuse to look at it.

When Tom returned home from work that night, we spoke not a word to each other. After dinner, he quietly went outside and began decapitating the demon. When next I went to check on his progress, the beast had been drawn and quartered, removed from my sight. It vanished as if it had never been. I felt elation, I felt guilt, but mostly, I felt drained. We continued our wordless battle for a further three days. The reason for my self-imposed silence was easy. I practiced one of the rules I taught my children—if I could not say anything nice, I would say nothing at all. I muttered those words repeatedly over the course of the next few days. It became my mantra.

Our voiceless conflict ended when I drew the curtain of anger and objectively viewed the reason for my outrage. While I pounded away on the computer keyboard, Ally arose from her slumber and sat on the floor beside my workstation. As she and I operated on the same wavelength, little introduction was required when I chose to speak. I blurted out, "Now I know why that canopy did what it did to me. It's all because of Corey."

Ally looked at me and replied, "Of course it is. Did you only just now figure that out?" She had known for days what I had determined only moments before. So wise for sixteen.

After spending days fumbling in the dark, I now found my world illuminated by a bright light. I finally understood and identified those three interwoven emotions that resided within me as if they were one entity—anger, frustration, and helplessness. Only then could I rationally speak to my husband and try to explain the reason for my most recent binge of anger. I was so quick to anger over such an inconsequential ugly thing that I did not stop to appreciate that perhaps it possessed some sort of value to him. As I listened to his plans for what was otherwise destined to become garbage, I finally understood his point of view. But why so angry, so frustrated? This, in turn, raised the complete feeling of helplessness. I could not move it, destroy it, or banish it from the yard. There was not a single thing I could do about it. These exact same feelings shot to the surface whenever I thought about Corey dying. I continued to be angry that it happened to him, frustrated because I did not know at whom I could direct my anger (the driver, the police, myself, my husband, the doctors, God), and I felt so damn helpless, because I still could not change the situation. The color of the canopy provided the pathway for so much emotion. Yellow had come to symbolize Corey. It was so plain, so simple, but so very complex.

For me, the ever-present hurt was so profound, so bottomless, and so deep that it could never heal. I suppose I may even have been guilty of choosing to keep my pain alive. It became a way for me to remember what happened to him and why he was no longer here. Otherwise, I feared I would forget him; he would be brushed aside and cast away as if he had never existed. I wonder now if he ever really lived, or was he a figment of my overactive imagination? That was when I touched the pain, remembered, and hurt. He must have lived, I concluded, because his death hurt so very much.

I remember when life was simple and easy to figure out. I remember when good days were termed good days and bad days were bad. Grief changed that definition. Now good days have become bad days and bad days are in fact good days. How can this be? For a grieving parent, a "bad day" would include forbidden things like crying, hurting, lethargy, and that compulsive need to talk. In actuality, those were my good days, as I allowed my son's death to penetrate my soul and look me dead square in the eye. When I felt like this, when I was forced to notice Corey's perpetual absence in my life, I tried to run. I performed amazing feats that the world would call therapeutic. I busied my hands and occupied my thoughts in an attempt to hold at bay those painful feelings. I have found this working on my grief to be very slow and not abundantly progressive or productive.

On the other side of the coin were the bad days, which the world would view as me having a "good day." Those were the days when I avoided grief. This was when my soul felt lighter, and dark thoughts were pushed aside. There was no need to cry, no need to wail. The glaring evidence that Corey was no longer here faded to the background. For that space in time, he was not here, and I accepted that fact. He could very well be off doing his own thing. But when he did not come home for dinner, when his car failed to appear in the driveway, grief slammed home. The hurt, therefore, could never leave me. The moments when I felt free of the burden were very rare indeed. It was always there, always waiting for me. Grief is very patient.

Over the years, I have been given proof beyond question that life does not end with death. It began with the reappearance of Rick in our lives and has grown to the point where strange phenomena are expected and not frightening at all. These episodes are not magnificent in manner nor are they obvious. They do however share the common thread of defying explanation and thankfully so.

By far, one of the most spectacular episodes we ever experienced came without warning. Tom arrived home late from work and, after eating dinner, headed upstairs to shower. About ten or fifteen minutes later, he called downstairs to me. As I climbed the stairs, I heard voices and music. I walked into our bedroom, where the noise became more pronounced with every step. Tom motioned me to look at the dresser. I could see a light coming from the partially opened top drawer. Corey's personal belongings—including his most treasured possession, a handheld portable color TV—were kept in there. He purchased it the year we went to Disneyland. As I peered into the drawer, my jaw dropped in wonder as I saw it was switched on. The volume was turned up, and the picture was clear even though the antenna was not raised.

I turned to Tom for an explanation as to why it was on. He had been in our room minutes before but said he had not opened the drawer. He said it was tightly shut when he plugged in his cell phone. So how did that TV get turned on?

Chapter Sixteen

The Essence of Grief

When I first began this project, I thought the hardest part would be starting. The most difficult part for me will be ending it, for there is no ending. My life continues on a day-to-day basis, and although it's not always pleasant, I am learning how to cope with a life that does not include Corey. I do not profess to know all the answers to this mystery, but I can promise that I will never stop searching. My quest in life is to try to understand why my child is no longer a living, breathing human being. Is he in a better place? I don't know, because this existence is the only one I know. My most profound hope and wish is that he is okay.

According to the laws of nature, parents die before their children. When you lose your parents, you lose your past. When you lose your child, you lose your future. As far as I am concerned, an addendum needs to be added to the laws of nature.

We attended Compassionate Friends meetings on a somewhat regular basis. We went with the intention of perhaps gaining insight into what other grieving parents were experiencing. I remember at more than one meeting expressing many doubts as to how Corey could be on that emergency-room table. From the corner of my eye, I saw many heads nodding in agreement. I was assured the one in denial was not me. I did not want my child to become another statistic. I did not want my child to die. I did not want my child standing at death's door, knowing there was no way out for him, that he had no choice, he had to die. These thoughts break my heart time and time again.

I am amazed at how much energy it takes to grieve. Who would have thought that one emotion like this could be so sapping? Outsiders may categorize this as feeling sorry for myself, but fortunately, I no longer care how I fit into their categories. I mentally shut down so that I can gather what precious resources I have to guide me through the next moment. And this has become my life. I will never be able to squander my energy. I can never run it down to the point where it dips into the red zone. I have come to know my limits.

One of the most heartfelt expressions anyone ever said to me is that they could not imagine what it means to lose a child. To me, this is the greatest form of acceptance. It is another person who has not experienced anything as devastating admitting that they cannot comprehend my grief.

So why am I writing this down? Why have I taken so many painful moments and compiled them together to present in a book? The answer to that arrived in the mail one day, and any doubt flew out the window.

That day, I casually leafed through the assortment of goodies the mailman brought our way. I came across a small card that bore the return address of the church where Corey's funeral service had been held. This puzzled me, for I could not understand why I would be receiving a card from them after all this time. I opened the thank-you card and read the following:

"Dear Tom, Karen, Jennifer, and Allison: You may remember me, my name is Peggy Hughes, and I *tried* to assist you in ways that I could for Corey's service. I cannot believe it was '94—it seems like a few months. Anyway, this note is to affirm the comments you wrote in Corey's memorial. You see, I could not understand them a year ago, and now I do.

"One night my husband, Tom, went to bed a healthy man and never woke up; this changed my life and that of our three daughters, and now we fully understand your comments and thank you for having the courage to write them. The public needs to hear them. Thank you.—Peggy Hughes."

This incredibly powerful message arrived as thoughts of resigning my position at work emerged, and the opportunity to begin composing my story came forth. How strange yet inspiring. Those words, "the public needs to know," became the motivation to push me forward on my mission.

Epilogue

At last we arrive at the epilogue. It surprises me to say that it has taken me three years to reach this final part of *Lost in Grief*. I have pondered what I should say, how to word it, where to start. In the end, I decided that writing from my heart was the only way to go.

In all likelihood, after making it safely across the finish line of my story, you are asking, "So, where are you today?" Because I choose not to plot my life on a timeline, I would have to say that I am here, a changed woman, a woman who still struggles with that one question: why? Over sixteen years later, I am still not any closer to solving that riddle. Why did this happen to us, to my family, and to me? Why did this happen to Corey?

If I were to ask any of Tom's family, they would lamely reply it was God's will. If I were to ask a priest, his reply would likely be the same. Direct this question to my husband, and his reply is silence. People say "God only knows," and I supposed He is the only one who truly does. I no longer ask *why* out loud. I silently propel my inquiry to the farthest reaches of the universe. It will take light years for my question to reach the source that possesses the answer, and light years for that reply to reach me. But by then, I will have long left this world for the next. Maybe that is where the answer lies. I have enough faith to know that I will receive an answer.

So is there any sort of hope I can offer someone, perhaps you, from where I stand? Well, first of all, I found there is always the hope that tomorrow will not be as black. There is the belief that perhaps the next breath will not hurt as much as the one previous. I found that if I looked inside myself, I could see my value as a human being. When I close my eyes, I allow the most precious things in life to infiltrate me, and it is my truest desire to pass them on to my son who can no longer experience them. Through me, he will recall walking on a pebble-strewn beach where each step is uncertain. When I feast my eyes upon a glorious sunrise or sunset, I find myself asking Corey if he can bear witness to the same spectacular sight. I describe to him the vivid reds, the succulent hues, the deepening shadows, the fading of the colors from the crystal-blue sky. When I hear the birds chattering to one another, I stop and listen even though I cannot understand a word they are saying. Perhaps Corey can. The gentle breeze I feel upon my skin is a kiss from heaven. When it ruffles my hair, the ends delightfully tickling my face, I find myself grinning like a child. Corey is responsible for that smile. As we speak the silent language we share, I look for signs from him, signals that he is in fact walking with me. Without this hope, I know I would truly doubt life. I believe he is around, and he always will be. The signs are everywhere. Tourmaline is his birthstone, cosmos is his birth flower, and blue is his favorite color.

The days blend together now with very little to mark one from the next. I do all the necessary things in life—take care of my family, tend to household chores, pay bills, cook the food, and purchase groceries. But all these things are done with a markedly different flavor. They are done when I can do them. I try not to let my housework pile up too high lest it become intimidating. Busyness is no longer a priority to me. There is more to life than keeping busy. There is the time to be still. I have learned how to be still while allowing the anxieties of day-to-day living to fall by the wayside.

I no longer wear a watch. Time, for me, has become something other than hands rotating around a face marked with numbers. I set my own pace, I mosey instead of rush. If I can, I do; if I can't, I don't. It is a luxury, this no longer suffering rule by the clock. I try to go with the flow of life and make adjustments along the way. At times, when I feel as if I have no direction at all, I inhale deeply and trust the angel I know is standing by my side.

Faith, trust, and love. But most of all, I believe.

So instead of trying to come up with words of wisdom, instead of trying to put into words the depth of pain I feel in my soul, I will tell you what I have learned.

I have learned that in order to *survive*, I have had to learn how to live. Giving up would have been so easy. I know because I did just that. But somehow, some way, Corey would not let me give up totally. Yes, I cried, I wailed, I begged, I pleaded, but nothing changed. I think it was necessary for me to do all those things just so that I could say I tried to change things through the only venue I knew: emotion. It also allowed me to get to the place where I am today. I think I can finally accept the fact that my son will not be coming home again. I don't like it, but there's nothing I can do to change it. I have also come to accept that life has many different faces—happiness, sadness, terror, joy, bewilderment, confusion, peacefulness, and grief. It took me fifteen long years to accept that life can be good even though I have seen the worst it has to offer. The moments of goodness are easy to recognize and appreciate. But I am profoundly more aware of how ugly my emotions can become. So I fight to stay alive, to find happiness in whatever I can, and when despair and anger set in, I no longer fight them. I allow despair, anger, and grief to wash over me, because I know they are only moments of raw emotion—emotion that should never be denied or ignored or worse, brushed aside. I am more in tune with what my feelings are saying and why it is I feel a certain way when ten seconds earlier, things were fine.

It takes a very long time to learn how to live again. I rebelled against that for many, many years. I didn't want to learn how to live again because if I did, that would mean that Corey meant nothing to me. I felt it was the least I could do for him—voluntarily surrender my life so that he would feel less alone in losing his. But my life isn't mine to give up. And it isn't up to me to say when my time on earth is through any more than it was for Corey. I am not speaking of suicide, because I don't believe that is the way to Corey. He came into our lives for only a short time. That is very difficult to admit and accept. And now that he is gone, our lives are forever changed. Corey changed my life for the better; his death changed my life in ways I never thought possible. And because of him, I am a much better person. Because of him, I got to experience life as a mom to an incredible young man. Because of him, I now appreciate nature as I never did before.

Karen Frenette

Do you know how hard you have to strain your ears to hear snow fall to the ground? Have you ever watched the sun rise from a place of darkness as it touches the tallest of trees before sliding its way downward and casting light on freshly formed dew, turning those droplets into nature's own diamonds? Have you ever heard the soft hooting of an owl at night in the middle of your own backyard? Have you ever truly listened to the language of the wind in the trees? Listen to what it is saying, embrace it and let it caress you. When life gets to be too much, I let nature take over and take me to places I have never been to before. And because Corey is nature, I will learn to trust again.

So, as it is said in the amateur radio world when ham operators sign off and bid farewell, I will follow suit and say, "73, my friends."

Afterword

I cannot truthfully say I have been consciously aware of the existence of guardian angels other than in the abstract sense, as I never had any real cause to believe. That has all changed now. Corey protects and guides me as he watches over my shoulder. He remains a constant in my life and in his family's life. I can feel his incredible sadness at being tragically and suddenly ripped away from us. He misses us as much as we miss him. I would welcome him home in whatever form if he was to return. That statement allowed me to open my heart to whatever shape he may assume, and these appearances are as varied as the weather.

Since Corey died, our family has been the recipient of many wonderful unearthly gifts. He lets us know he is still around, and although I never hear his voice, I have become very good at recognizing him. In addition to warm chills, I have also experienced phenomena that would normally be unexplainable or regarded as nothing more than coincidence. But there is no such thing as coincidence. Things have happened to me that include everything from lights flashing on their own to mysterious, story-like dreams.

Corey had a way with animals. He was particularly fond of Cleo, Jenn's cat. Cleo was extremely fussy about who received her affection. She would give hugs—this little fur ball would actually embrace the person by placing one paw on each shoulder and laying her head on the chest. The amazing thing is she only did this to two people: Corey and Jennifer. Ally tried, but Cleo would not comply.

Jenn told me a story about Cleo pacing in front of the closet where we kept Corey's belongings. Cleo incessantly meowed and would not let up until Jenn moved the dresser that blocked the closet and opened the door. Jenn called down for me to witness her cat. I peeked inside the closet and there she was, curled up on the floor, purring for all she was worth. She looked up at the trunk that towered over her, eventually jumping up and tucking herself into the farthest reaches of that cramped space. She just sat there contentedly purring, and every once in a while, she would arch her back and rub up against Corey's jacket that hung in the closet. It seemed that she too needed her "Corey fix," and when finished, she jumped down off the trunk and left the room.

While I was working on the computer, Cleo came around my chair, purring as she looked up at me. I called to her, giving her permission to jump up on my lap. She promptly got comfortable, purring all the while. At one point, she put her paws on the keyboard, jumped up on the desk, and leaned into the joystick Corey once used. When Jenn saw the manner in which her cat acted, she told me more strange behaviors that Cleo had demonstrated.

As before, Cleo entered Jenn's room and began meowing in such a fashion that Jenn stopped what she was doing and paid attention to her cat. Cleo approached the closet, looked at Jenn, and meowed. Jenn knew what she was after—she needed her Corey fix. Cleo stood by the closet door, looking it up and down, when suddenly she ran from the door frightened by something. Once a safe distance on the other side of the room, she locked her eyes on that door as she tried to stare it down. Jenn moved all the stuff blocking access to the closet and opened the door for her. Cleo entered and jumped up on the trunk. Jenn listened as Cleo sniffed around. Finally, content that all was in order, she comfortably settled herself into place and began purring once again. What made this particular incident bizarre was that this cat never went into any other closet in the house. How did she know Corey's stuff was in there?

I may not know much about the intuitive nature of animals, but I do know that this cat was in tune with the unseen world. She missed Corey as much as the rest of us. Her way of coping and understanding was not much different from humans'. She liked her own space and always made it known we should be thankful for her presence. Since Corey died, she began acting incredibly human. She would sit for hours on the computer chair where he used to sit. Even her meow became unusual. In the past, she had always had a very soft voice, but it then transformed into a yowl. Do cats keen?

Dreams were another way in which Corey reached out to us. What are dreams? Are they manifestations of something we desire or are they real? Do they exist for only a moment and then disappear, never to be thought of or remembered again? Or are they actually a moment in time when our minds are unburdened and therefore receptive to messages and communication? Can these be a form of mail—d-mail, perhaps?

My dreams of Corey have always been welcome, even though they are painful. They have ranged from seeing him as a baby to sitting down and talking to a wizened old man. I recall asking him how I was to know who he was, and he told me, "You'll know." And I have. When I dream of him, it always involves touching his curly unruly hair and exchanging a warm hug. I recall asking him where he had gone to, and the reply I received involved a red wagon he had built. Attached to the sides of the wagon were countless little cards. The card on top had Corey's name written on it, and beneath that was an inscription. It read, "I'm gone where the trains go when you cannot see them anymore and where the rainbows are (up in the sky)."

Some dreams last longer than others, and when they do, a story is told.

I dreamed it was the middle of the day. Noise and activity in the house were at an all-time high, so I decided to head out to the shed to do some transplanting where I could look forward to some peace and quiet. As much as I loved my family, sometimes solitude was a necessary evil. I entered my sanctuary and placed three green plastic pots on the bench and began a search for my mixture of potting soil and vermiculite. I reached inside the bag and pulled out three sticks. How peculiar. Even though I knew I was dreaming, I vividly recalled the memory of the time when Corey planted three sticks in his sandbox when he was only three years old.

Suddenly, I turned to the doorway and found Corey standing there. Clasped in his hand was a blue binder. I waved the sticks at him and said, "I want some peace and quiet. No kids allowed." He silently stood there, not uttering a word. Perhaps it was the look on his face, or maybe my heart thought better of those words. I set the sticks aside and told him he could stay. I asked him, "Do you miss your life the way it was?"

He replied, "Yeah, I do. Now people act as if I do not exist. It is like they do not see me."

I thought to myself, *They can't.*

He then said, "I do not understand that thing that happened to my head."

I was at a loss as to what I should say, so I chose to say nothing instead. After a pause, I asked him what he had in his hand, for the binder had transformed into some sort of electrical box or mini electrical panel.

He said, "This is something I built about two years ago." He had been working on a project for a family friend but never completed it, and it sat unfinished on Bill's desk as a reminder of Corey. As he spoke, I stared at his hands, transfixed. The skin was shredded around the cuticles like it had always been. Then I saw the little scar on his left index finger. Corey was back, and my heart filled with joyous wonder. But at that particular moment, I could feel the dream ending, as I was pulled away from him and back to reality.

Our backyard has always been a sanctuary for me. It was only natural that Corey chose this place to meet me the next night. I felt the love surrounding me as I stood there, clearly recalling how Corey explained to me about the massive project he needed to complete involving four separate, distinct parts. One part had an artistic component to it; another involved a written essay; the third involved building something; while the fourth and final part was never revealed to me. He explained that each segment would take approximately two hours to complete, with a total allowable time of eight hours. He began to panic, because he felt there would not be enough time to accomplish this. I told him what we always tried to teach him—one step at a time. I looked around as I reminded him of this and only then did I notice the incredible colors surrounding me. The sky was a breathtaking blue, and the lawn was an amazing vibrant shade of green. I can still recall to this day the sense of completeness I felt at that moment as I became a whole person once again.

I am not the only one to have such dreams. It was wonderful to hear that Corey connected with his dad. Tom dreamed that the five of us were in Toronto, Ontario, on a subway train. We sat close together in the same coach. Suddenly, a disabled person boarded the train and began looking for a place to sit. He asked if one of us would mind giving up our seat. Corey jumped to his feet and said he would be more than happy to move. He then turned to his dad saying he would find another place to sit on the train and not to worry. Before leaving, Tom asked him if he knew the name of the station where we planned to exit. After giving reassurance to his dad, Corey disappeared into the next car. We reached our destination, left the train, and began our search for Corey. Panic began to settle in as Tom realized Corey was nowhere to be found. He called his name, searching every face in the crowd. Surely someone must have seen him. As the train pulled away from the station, Tom knew in his heart that Corey had stayed on and left. I remembered then the dream I had when he told me he was gone where the trains go when you can't see them anymore. How heartbreakingly sad.

As with all stories, three dreams have stayed with me. I have entitled them "The Stairway to Heaven," "Found and Lost," and "The Separation between You and I."

The Stairway to Heaven

I found myself standing beside some red iron stairs. Someone stood behind me on my right. I turned around and there was Corey, sporting the same clothes he wore when he died, smiling the same half-smile he would always have on his face when he was glad to see you. I looked at him, and we immediately embraced; I proceeded to give him one of his old hugs, the kind where one arm is slung around the shoulders while the opposite sides of the body touch. He instantly recognized what I was doing and said, "I thought I taught you better than that." Those were the same words I spoke to him as I taught him what a real hug involved. He embraced me and squeezed me so hard that I could feel him crushing the breath from my lungs. He released me, and as I turned to go, I saw him begin ascending the red iron stairs. Were these the stairs that led to heaven? I asked him if he was going to accompany me but he said, "No, I have to go this way."

Found and Lost

A young child appeared on my doorstep, naked and shivering. Not knowing to whom this child belonged, I brought him in, wondering if maybe he had simply wandered away from one of the houses in the neighborhood. This certainly didn't explain his lack of clothing. I clothed him, fed him, and tended to him. My front door remained wide open, as I fully expected someone would show up looking for this child. I asked him if he was tired, if he would like to take a nap. His little face lit up as he answered, "Yes." I carried him upstairs and tucked him in my bed. I returned to my station at the front door when I noticed a family coming up the road. Maybe they were looking for the lost child. I waited in breathless expectation for them to come up the driveway, eagerly anticipating the joy on their faces when I was able to reunite them with their missing son. Instead, they kept on walking past my house. My heart sank for this poor little orphan.

Suddenly I no longer was in the house but down the road watching as a Volkswagen car drove erratically up our street. I instantly knew that the driver was after the little boy. I felt deep and profound fear. I ran as I followed the car up the road and watched as it parked across the street from my house. A man got out of the car and approached our home. I could only think, *How did he find the boy? Out of all the houses, how did he manage to find the place where this child sought refuge?*

He walked toward the house and then went back to his vehicle several times, as if undecided. On his final return to his vehicle, he pulled a blanket from the car. He had to know the child had no clothing. I watched helplessly as this person went up the walkway, entered the house without knocking, ascended the stairs, and took the child.

The scene then changed to the back door of our house. The child was very complacent, as if drugged. He did not fight this man. I turned to Corey and told him to warm up the van, as we would need to follow this person to see where he was going. Corey was standing behind the man when suddenly the child vanished. Corey tried to say something while attempting to distract this person before he left the house. I asked Corey what he wanted, and he said, "Call the police." Corey left with this man as I ran upstairs to dial 911. The phone would not work. There was no dial tone. I began to panic. I tried again but nothing; it still would not work. I reached over to turn on the light, and as I did, I begged that the phone would work. When I tried to dial again, it functioned, but the line was full of static. I connected with a lady and gave her the information. She confirmed our address and said, "Someone will be right there. This is a lead and therefore important." It was then that I heard Jenn on the other line as she screamed. I hung up the phone. I did not want anyone to know I had called for help. A man dressed in black suddenly appeared behind me, whereupon I woke up. I could not shake the feeling that I had come face to face with the grim reaper.

The Separation between You and I

When people enter our home, they rarely use the front door, opting instead for the less formal side-door entry or carport door. In my dream, I passed through the playroom/computer room on my way to the kitchen. The carport door is located on the right-hand side. As I exited the room, I looked to my right and there stood Corey, behind the closed door. The strange part was that the glass was missing and the curtain was pushed aside. He stood propped against the door frame, smiling his lazy, relaxed Corey smile. He wore his blue BUM shirt as he stood there grinning at me with obvious amusement. I have never felt such unrestrained joy in my life. I could actually feel my jaw dropping as I deeply inhaled. I motioned with my hand for him to come in. I said, "You came back. You're here!" and he smiled while nodding yes. I wanted so much to find Tom, but I felt extreme reluctance to move my feet. I knew that if I glanced away, even for just a moment, he would vanish. As I watched in abject fascination, Corey began to fade before my very eyes, and in that moment, I knew that the only thing separating me from that place where we will all go one day was my lack of imagination. Remove the glass and push aside the curtain, and Corey would be right there.

Ironically, this dream occurred on Mother's Day, 1997.

About the Author

What makes a good storyteller? A good weaver of tales possesses the ability to paint a picture so vivid and intriguing that the reader cannot turn away. I believe that the best storytellers of nonfiction are those who have walked through fire. My personal fire is something no parent should ever experience. It simply goes against the laws of nature.

There are very few courses of learning in which you are first handed a certificate and subsequently embark upon an intimate learning journey regarding the subject of the certificate. Such is the case when you hold in your hand your child's death certificate. To call it every mother's worst nightmare is to be kind. You can awaken from a nightmare. The very substance that holds your thoughts and your soul together abandons you. You are stripped naked of all pretenses held in your former life. What is left is bound and gagged, and you are cast out into a world cold with the indifference that the innocence of others affords. You are fed a cruel diet, a litany of euphemisms, used by what we have come to call *the others* so that they can ward off the horrifying contagion you now carry. "At least he didn't suffer." "It was God's will." "Forgiveness will set you free." "Life is for the living." "Life goes on." To be honest, it doesn't. In one ill-fated second, it stops. You die when your child dies. Only you are reborn, helpless and nearly lifeless—an infant born into a living nightmare. You struggle to breathe, fighting to survive with only one searing, all-consuming question that will devour you. That question is "Why?" They say there are seven stages of grief. "They" are usually university-trained professionals who studied the subject of grief. Some have written books on it. "They," however, are *the others* whose learned truths ring hollow to those who have lived that same truth. What they do not say is that the stages of grief do not come in any particular order or that they can last any length of time and that you can experience a stage any number of times. They do not say that any stage may succeed in crushing the breath and indeed the very life from you.

When the world I had nurtured for so long was shattered by the senseless death of my only son, I clung desperately to any source of comfort. For a time, I turned to the world of books to find some insight, any clues into this new life I would now lead. My search for solace left me feeling empty. How many parents have had to endure the death of a child? What are their thoughts, their feelings, their stories? A suggestion early on in my journey led me to where I am today. Fuelled by the burning question "Why?" I tried to claw my way to the surface of life; nothing would connect, nothing would stick. I could not rebuild my life as I was told I must, because who I was had become a series of random dots with nothing connecting them. Someone said, "Write it down." Desperate to cling to any hope, I began to journal, intermittently at first and then building slowly until my need to journal became an obsession. At last I found an audience for all of my most private feelings. There was now something with which I could share my deepest and darkest moments of despair—the fever pitch of my anger, the random attacks of relentless sobbing. That I would ever share these intimate revelations with another soul never crossed my mind. My journals were simply my lifeline along which I could climb, hand over hand, to each new level of my new and frightening reality. So I wrote until the words tumbled from me. I filled volumes. Then one day, several years later, I stopped. It was not until a passage of time that I was able to return to those volumes. As I descended into fears and feelings I thought I had left behind, I would revisit my first encounters with those feelings. I would identify with those earlier thoughts. From them I could, I found, actually draw comfort, a feeling that I was not alone. Out of those thoughts was born the seed that blossomed into *Lost in Grief*. I knew that if these words could comfort me, it was a human compassionate necessity that I collect these thoughts, refine them, and share them. I felt that if my words could reach out and touch the soul of one person and make a positive difference by handing them a silver thread of hope, I must do it.

I have spent the last ten years analyzing, writing, and rewriting my thoughts so I could reach out today, silver thread in hand.

I continue to survive on Vancouver Island with my husband, Tom, and our ever caring, ever faithful, ever patient companion Maggie, our two-year-old yellow lab.

With our two daughters now blessing our lives with beautiful grandchildren, I am taken back to my own beginnings. I can now allow myself to achingly enjoy the memories of when our children were young and life was *normal*.

CPSIA information can be obtained at www.ICGtesting.com
Printed in the USA
LVOW061812130613

338486LV00005B/287/P